IN SEARCH OF EVERLASTING JOY

Notes of A Materialistic Man

ARUN BÉHAL

Made with ♥ on the Notion Press Platform
www.notionpress.com

This book is not intended as a commercial project.
Any proceeds earned by the author from its sale will be donated to charity.

CONTENTS

		Page No.
Chapter 1:	**The Quest for the Right Ideology**	1
	Malow's Hierarchy of needs	
Chapter 2:	**The Theory of Inner Joy**	11
Chapter 3:	**The Technique**	15
	What is yoga?	
	Why do you need skill to perform actions?	
Chapter 4:	**Steps for the Practice of Yoga**	22
Chapter 5:	**Self-Awareness**	25
	AtmaShatkam	
Chapter 6:	**Spell of Ignorance**	31
	Maya	
	Ego	
	Am I the doer?	
Chapter 7:	**A Man of Stable Wisdom**	38
Chapter 8:	**Trap of Desires and Senses**	40
	Desires and senses	
Chapter 9:	**Route to Joy - Vairagya**	46
	Demystifying *Vairagya*	
Chapter 10:	**Insight on Karma**	56
	The spiritual dimension of karma	
	Butcher's Gita	

The Dilemma of Selfless Work
Dharma
Swadharma

Chapter 11:   **Divine Wisdom**   70
Knowledge and Divine Wisdom

Chapter 12:   **Devotion (Bhakti)**   72
Is devotion just superstition?
Distortion in religious institutions
Mukti (Liberation)

Chapter 13:   **Karma Yoga of Squirrel**   80

Chapter 14:   **The Science of Yoga**   85
Mental Faculty
Discipline of Yoga

Chapter 15:   **The Yoga Tool Kit**   89
Determination
Knowledge of three modes of nature:
Discrimination (Vivek)
Tolerance towards the pair of opposites
Friendly and compassionate
Contentment
Moderation
Pranayama
Food
Hatha Yoga
Meditation

Chapter 16:   **Yoga – Why?**   99
Why should one follow yoga?
Cost of effort
Emotional Intelligence
Bondages of Action (Karmabandhan)

Protection from fear
Clarity of mind
Health
Productivity

Chapter 17:   **Challenges on the Path of Yoga**   106
Search for Happiness: Mindless is
restless, and craving
Ahankara
Attachments
Yogi is rare
Remedy

Am I a Yogi? – A Checklist   112

Conclusion   113

1.

THE QUEST FOR THE RIGHT IDEOLOGY

I have this life, and I want to make the most of it. I want to enjoy it!

We all want to be happy. Happiness and a good life are universal goals. Everyone keeps looking for it throughout life.

Parents and well-wishers instil in us the idea that life without wealth, power, and status is a struggle and a drudgery from a young age. The concept becomes more concrete as we observe the world and mature. We notice wealthy people around us enjoy the comforts of life, whereas poor or hand-to-mouth people face hardships. The rich and powerful get respect and have access to other rich and powerful people running the affairs of the social system, further enhancing their sphere of influence. On the other hand, the underprivileged remain marginalised. We see people living life worse than animals. There is no doubt that the teachings of our parents and our learning about the importance of wealth have a lot of substance. It is essential for any person to consider this concept seriously. In addition to the quest for money and power, we possess an innate instinct for sense pleasure.

What are we seeking? Why is lasting happiness elusive? What obstacles prevent us from feeling content? Defining a fulfilling life poses intricate challenges.

A normal man doesn't even know what brings happiness. Does happiness lie in thrills or peace? But had happiness been the only outcome of wealth, power, status, or even sense pleasure, it could have reduced the complexity. Had it been clear what makes us happy, the quest for the right approach could not have continued even after the ages of human civilisation.

"Mortals can never be happy with wealth," asserts Nachiketa to the lord of death, Yamaraj, while refusing his offer for various types of pleasures along with the kingdom of the world in lieu of Nachiketa's demand for knowledge about the truth of death.

When Nachiketa, a mere boy in Katha Upanishad, countered Yamraj with the logic of vanity for wealth and pleasures, Yamaraj couldn't refute it.

A few wise and lucky people, after spending a considerable life span, realise the insignificance of all the pleasures of the world for overall happiness and fulfilment. The great majority are oblivious to it till the end. Man remains on a roller-coaster ride that alternates between highs, success, and pleasure, as well as lows, failure, and suffering.

Everyone has to do some work to maintain this body and to pay for the cost of comfort and enjoyment. We are part of society, which is also an emotional requirement, and there are various norms for those who are part of this social system. Enjoyment, too, comes from a variety of sources: fun, thrills, success, sex, status, love, kids, position, and the list goes on. Some also rely on alcohol or even drugs in the same pursuit. They also draw their own logical inferences based on their experience. There is no need to elaborate on how long such conviction or illusion lasts and the irreparable damage associated with it.

Each man also has responsibilities for the welfare of his family and himself. There are moral obligations. And there is so much to do! There is so much to accomplish and enjoy. One is desperately looking for means to be secure. He has to earn respect.

In this backdrop, the classification of human needs by Maslow in 1943 is a valuable contribution.

Maslow's hierarchy of 'needs':

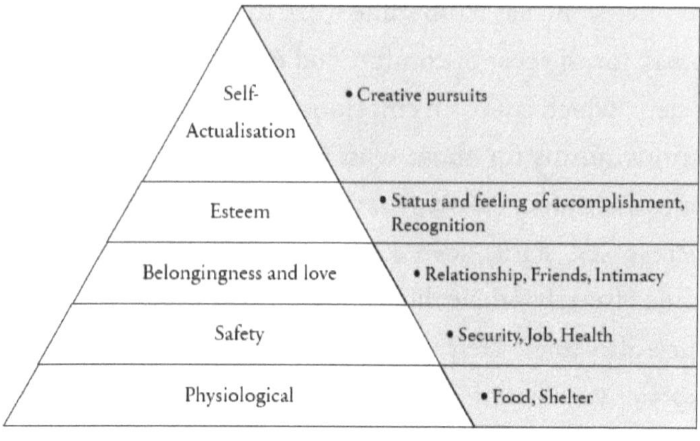

The initial concept in this important psychology theory was to classify human needs in a hierarchy with the concept that after needs at the lower level get satisfied, then needs at the next level arise. Maslow's theory was later amended to acknowledge that needs at all levels exist simultaneously and overlap each other, but intensity may vary depending upon the situation and personality of an individual. Every human need all these to live! It is an engagement for the whole life, as one or another element keeps missing. As one grows up, he gets into a never-ending chase, depleting his precious life energy. At the same time, one can't just give up and retire for peace. Whoever defies standards set by society is considered lazy and irresponsible, and he pays a price for it. That is also not enough because, even after being easy-going, one fails to experience happiness and peace.

The fundamental needs are clear-cut, but the man born with the most advanced brain among all living things on earth suffers further harm from ego and self-fulfilment needs, which increase stress, anxiety, frustration, and other depressive thoughts. Man suffers because of his emotions, distorted thinking, and overthinking, which create lots of emotional charge, having not only an adverse impact on health but also depriving one of the feeling of joy. Overthinking, worries, and fears dominate even during fun activities. At the most, one can take his mind off these for a short span of time.

Right ideology

Being sensitive and ambitious is disastrous, and its impact is severe on physical and emotional health. Unless life is structured on the foundation of the right ideology, it is certain to crumble at some stage. The world has always been volatile, uncertain, complex, and ambiguous (VUCA), emphasising the challenges of navigating such an environment. There is no guarantee that everything will go the way one wants. One has to work and face hardships, but the mind wants to avoid difficulties and enjoy comforts. Life is replete with unexpected twists and formidable challenges. With success, there are failures too. One can't always succeed. No one can be happy all the time, and difficulties are bound to come later or sooner.

Philosophers and religious leaders have erupted across the globe to give solace to masses chasing happiness with techniques and beliefs to live and die with, either in the name of religion or lifestyle concepts.

Man, in the search of peace and a meaningful life, takes refuge in spirituality but often remains confused between spirituality and the real-life demand for materialism. The term materialism implies inferior values in comparison to spiritualism. But in real-life drama, the practical requirements of life and our natural instincts take priority. We are brought up to work to earn a living, support our families, be prosperous to improve our lifestyle, status, and recognition, fight for survival in tough cut-throat competition, and enjoy. On the other hand, there is a road to spirituality, which is an inward journey either in quest for peace or realisation of God, or both.

Spirituality and materialism are both indispensable for a holistic life. Walking on a mere spiritual path is very difficult for a normal man. It may be feasible for only a few to live a retired life without financial worries before old age. A very few also give up worldly aspiration and choose to become monks, saints, etc. in the true sense. But still, one remains engaged in all sorts of actions. However, at the same time, worldly pursuits without spiritual awareness and practice can be devastating.

Any thinking individual struggles with many basic questions for self-management. The value system teaches us to be good, and so is the expectation of society from us. What is the definition of being good? Is being good a way to let people take advantage of us? Is cunningness necessary to succeed? Do we accumulate sins while doing so? What is peace or happiness? How can it be achieved? How should we live a meaningful life? Will I repent at the moment of death that I wasted my life in unnecessary pursuits?

Each man has his own struggle, which for him is the biggest battle being fought in his lifetime. Everyone needs to upskill himself not only for struggle but also to master peace, as it is also an essential dimension of life and the core requirement of our soul, which takes the maximum toll in the struggle of life. Only a few wise people know the art of being in joy amidst chaos and uncertainty in life.

The ultimate skill was taught by Sri Krishan at an extreme juncture of life and death to his friend Arjun, who was the most ferocious warrior of the otherwise comparatively weak Pandavas army. When the war was about to begin, right on the battlefield, perplexed by the outcome, Arjun surprised everyone. He put down his weapons and bowed before his friend performing as a charioteer, Sri Krishan, with the declaration, "I will not fight."

It was a war of the magnitude of the world war of that time, as most of the prominent kings were committed to fighting on either side of both cousins - the Pandavas or the Kauravs. These warriors possessed weapons of mass destruction, which could have changed the face of the earth. Even after 5000 years, Sri Krishan's words of wisdom have served as mankind's most priceless asset and saviour. The observations on human nature, our understanding of our existence, and the technique of yoga are as relevant in modern times as they were thousands of years ago. This is the power of the Bhagavad Gita. It is accepted as the essence of Hindu philosophy amidst the myriad of scriptures evolved over the centuries of research by the enlightened sages. The Gita is a practical book of human psychology that addresses the limitations and weaknesses of human nature, which force us away from the restful state of mind.

Hindus have various sects and believe in different forms of worship. But even those who do not worship Sri Krishan as the ultimate God read and follow the Gita with the same reverence. Even believers of other religions find a lot of solace and answers in the Gita. The philosophy of the Gita, as discussed in the later part of this book, has a significant place for devotion. But these principles of devotion do not necessarily contradict any religious belief or pose a threat to the practice of any religion. It will not be incorrect to conclude that the Bhagavad Gita is above religion and essentially a self-help book that has been in use for centuries.

Just one cursory reading makes one realise that Gita is the remedy leading to peace without giving up the world or responsibilities to be carefree. As I was growing up, I observed holy men lecturing on the Gita in temples, giving the impression that it was a religious text. No doubt it is. But it is also much more than that.

In contrast to what appeared to be only lessons about renunciation and austerity, serious study taught me how to seize the bull by its horns. Rather than running away in the name of renunciation, the Gita urges active engagement in life's challenges.

My belief is strengthened by contemplating the anchor, Sri Krishan, who is a symbol of cheerfulness and love. He is charming, pleasant, playful, and full of life in every sphere. There is nothing sad about him. He has struggled with one or another issue throughout his life. Secondly, the whole objective of the Gita is to propel Arjun to fight the war to take back the kingdom belonging to his family from his cousins, even though his most beloved grandfather was fighting from the other side. The teachings are to motivate Arjun to give up thoughts of quitting and instead fight the war. Arjun didn't start singing the glory of God on the battlefield or meditating, but he took up the fight for his rights to take revenge for the insult to his wife. The background of the Battle of Mahabharat was very complex. Each side gave strong reasons to justify their actions or stands. From another's perspective, what one person considered to be a misdeed or an exploitation could actually be the right course of action.

Arjun concluded that the war was immoral as it amounted to killing his own cousins, elders, and teachers for kingdom and wealth. He was so emotionally drained to see his grandfather and teachers as opponents that he was ready to beg to eat rather than kill them to regain the kingdom. In such a tough situation, Sri Krishan taught him, from a philosophical and practical point of view, how to face the conflicting situations. This is the reason behind the popularity of the Gita. It is a path to resolve the dilemmas of life through the eternal principles governing humans. The Gita teaches through constructive dialogue to clear doubts arising out of the intricacies of the spiritual teachings. Such constructive discussions are promoted in Hinduism to establish concepts in mind based on inquiry and clarifications rather than mere repetitions or blind following. The followers mature their fundamental understanding with time, personal experiences, readings, and interactions with learned people.

Mesmerised by the glory of the Bhagavad Gita, this book is based on its everlasting wisdom to answer some of the basic questions I faced. I started reading the Gita when I was young, and the teachings of the Gita have played such a significant role in my life that they have repeatedly saved me from trying circumstances. It put me on track whenever I got haywire due to my inbuilt lower instincts. It may also sound strange that my interpretation of the core message of Gita has also undergone change many times. There are various commentaries by highly qualified and learned people on the subject, and many of these carry different impressions.

I admit that I am still a student and, as said in the title, 'a materialistic man'. The effort here is to find the best way to live and enjoy life without losing its purpose. It is crucial to determine what constitutes a meaningful life instead of being caught in a perpetual pursuit and conforming to societal norms. As this book aims to explore joy, peace, and happiness, let's delve into uncovering the science of happiness.

2.

THE THEORY OF INNER JOY

That night, my cousin, who frequently visited Delhi for business trips, was staying with us. Around midnight, my mother woke me up as my father was not feeling well. Though initially I felt it could be minor acidity, we decided to visit the hospital. On reaching the hospital, the doctor could diagnose in no time that my father was having a massive heart attack, and he was immediately admitted to the ICU. This was the first time in my life that I visited an ICU ward of any hospital. The experience left me in a state of profound numbness, unable to process the situation. But my cousin, who accompanied me, was a tough man. He managed the situation. After watching an occasional straight line on the monitor in the ICU, my father recovered, and the doctor prescribed him bypass surgery as he had blockage in his arteries. That was the time when I started looking for information on heart disease and came across a book by Dr. Dean Ornish - Program for Reversing Heart Disease.

Despite years of exploring spirituality, I believe this book was pivotal in clarifying fundamental spiritual principles for me. The recommendation from the renowned western doctor gave me the conviction to experiment with the insightful concepts uncovered in this book, which is otherwise accessible to anyone born into traditional Hindu families. However, religious practices in my family were limited to performing prayers twice a day, visiting temples regularly, and focusing on good karma.

Dr. Dean Ornish revealed in his book that he was facing pressure from studies during his college life to the extent that he developed suicidal thoughts. At that point, through his sister, he got introduced to Swami Satchidananda, a spiritual teacher who introduced him to techniques to discover a happier life. Swami initiated dispelling wisdom with the concept *that nothing can ever bring you everlasting happiness*. He learned the fundamental principle that *happiness is already there*; all it requires is to quieten the constant chattering mind to experience inner peace, and it is a self-defeating notion that power and happiness come from getting more and more wants and needs fulfilled. He goes to the extent of declaring that his book, Programme for Reversing Heart Disease, has the core concept that *lasting peace and happiness is not something to get, but we already have it, until disturbed.*

My further learnings on the subject repeatedly emphasised that until one continues to look for happiness in worldly subjects, objects, or people, happiness will definitely continue to play hide and seek with him.

> ***Natural happiness is not something to seek for, it is always there unless we disturb it.***

Moreover, living beings by nature are incomplete and, hence, restless. The mind wanders around in search of comfort, which is much more than physical comfort for the body. One can notice it in the analysis of one's thought patterns. Due to experience of the past or even present life, when one comes across such a movement of pleasure, he continues to crave for the same again and again. But this happiness fades after some time. The vicious circle continues not only lifelong but from one life to another. This attachment or possessiveness to what pleases creates fear of loss and, hence, insecurities. Pure joy remains elusive. There is no guilt about it, as it is a natural aspect of human existence. No one likes hardships.

However, with an understanding of what real happiness is, one starts moving in the right direction, towards inner joy, which ultimately pleases and is actually required.

Maharshi Patanjali identified five causes of suffering in humans: *Avidya* (Ignorance), *Asmita* (Egoism), *Raag* (Attachments, obsessions), *Devesh* (Aversion, hate), and *Abhinivesha* (desire to cling to life—fear of death and will to live). (Patanjali Yog Sutra 2.3).

These causes are rooted in internal factors and necessitate a transformation from within.

The paradigm shift happens the moment one realises the temporary nature of worldly pleasures and starts relying on inner joy. This approach triggers a change in overall life. Then one starts making efforts not to disturb the inner joy and natural bliss, which is not in chasing happiness but in cessation of cravings or aversions. The realisation that *Kamana* (lust) or ego does not give everlasting pleasure kills the requirement for unnecessary pursuits. Such awareness not only fosters acceptance of adversities but also diminishes attachment to favourable circumstances or outcomes.

Inner joy or eternal pleasure comes from the right knowledge, discipline, and discrimination to stay away from obsessions or aversions.

Easier said than done!

The ancient Indian scriptures, such as the Bhagavad Gita and the Yog Vashist, have delved into profound questions that transcend mere religious boundaries, offering insights into a deeper quest for human meaning at the psychological level. In the Bhagavad Gita, Sri Krishan, the divine, guides his friend Arjun, whereas in the Yog Vashisht, the mentor and sage, Rishi Vashisht, answers the question of Lord Ram.

3.

THE TECHNIQUE

Let's focus on ways to stop the chattering mind to experience happiness. One way is to go to a secluded place and live a quiet life. Can monasteries or ashrams truly offer a solution? Silencing the mind appears simple, but its application in a real time scenario is a frustrating exercise. The mind remains filled with uncontrollable noises due to various reasons. Even retiring to mountains, ashrams, or secluded places may somewhat reduce it, but it remains elusive without adopting a holistic approach encompassing all dimensions of life. It is not only selfish but also fails to deliver peace in the long run in most cases. Moreover, is it truly practical to sacrifice a conventional lifestyle in pursuit of inner peace? Is there another way to find harmony within daily routines?

In this backdrop, the principle of Sri Krishan's yoga is the remedy for those who are overwhelmed with the complexity of such questions but desperately need peace and miss the feeling of joy. Krishan also exposes how futile it is to cut off and the pitfalls of the strategy of giving up actions. The discussion between Sri Krishan and Arjun unfolds many life-changing secrets, but overall, Sri Krishan insists on Arjun following the path of action with the technique of yoga:

Yogasthau kuru karmani, saigaa tyktva Dhanajaya
siddhy- asiddhyou samo bhutva, samatvaa yoga ucyate

Perform actions established in yoga, renouncing attachments, Dhananjya (Arjun)! Equipoised in achievement / success, or failure (of efforts), equanimity is called yoga. *(BG 2.48).*

Each word in the succinct poetic narration of the Bhagavad Gita carries weight. The message in the above verse can be dissected as:

1. Established in yoga, perform actions
2. Give up attachments.
3. Be the same in success and failure.
4. Being the same (equipoised) is called yoga.

Though action is the valuable message of the Bhagavad Gita, the concept is complete only when this action is performed skilfully without attachments and equanimity, i.e., getting over a storm of emotions.

This holistic technique of Sri Krishn is called yoga. Though Sri Krishan repeatedly emphasised yoga during his conversation with Arjun, what yoga is remains hidden.

The Bhagavad Gita has 18 chapters, and the first chapter just sets the background. The second chapter is like an executive summary of the Gita. In a way, the Gita is over in the second chapter. The remaining chapters are supporting material to satisfy the queries of Arjun, because he is the main warrior in the battle and seeker of wisdom. Sri Krishan is a friend and just a charioteer who took a vow not to take up arms in this war. He is the symbol of wisdom and divine power. Arjun, in despair, bows down to him, not to anyone else, for the right guidance. His brothers were standing with him. His beloved grandfather and master (teacher), though fighting from the other side, still had immense love for him and were also present on the battlefield. But Arjun took refuge in the source of wisdom. This also depicts that, in real life too, divine knowledge is the ultimate friend and saviour of anyone in difficult situations if he surrenders to the ultimate power and seeks guidance. Another cue here is that the divine will not act on behalf of anyone but rather provide guidance to one who surrenders to him and asks for his blessings. Divine may assist indirectly, but everyone has to make efforts.

My personal book of life, the Bhagavad Gita, for simplification and easy reminder, is summed up in just three words of this verse: *Yogasthau Kuru Karmani: Established in yoga, perform your work.* The rest, for me, is the elaboration of the concept and toolkit.

What is yoga?

In a nutshell, yoga is the central essence of the Bhagavad Gita, which is a remedy to conflicting issues and a path of freedom without being irresponsible. The concept of yoga, introduced in the beginning, remains the central theme, as Sri Krishan stresses again and again throughout the Gita to follow the path of yoga.

"Be a yogi!" he insists. So, it is important to begin with understanding: What, after all, is this yoga?

Often, yoga is linked to its popular version of physical exercise and postures, whereas yoga of the Gita is much deeper. The actual word yoga means to join. The root meaning of *yog* is the state of union, combination, addition, or co-existence. In astrology, *a yog* is a combination of planets. *Yog* is also a trick *(Yukti):* the technique to combine or mix different concepts to find a way out of a complex situation.

Therefore, Yog in the Gita is the skill to perform work: *Yoga Karaya Kuasulam (BG 2:50).* The Yoga of the Gita can be understood as a skilled way of doing work while maintaining equanimity or peace of mind. *It is a technique, as yoga is also the state of severance from contact with sorrow (BG 6.23).*

This is the foundation concept of Gita, which often gets lost in the various other life changing theories and mystic revelations in the book. Equanimity of mind stands out as the most crucial aspect among all other techniques or logical explanations in the Gita. It seems simple, but the whole Gita is an attempt to answer various questions to clarify the fundamental concepts in order to achieve this goal. Equanimity is not something that can be forced upon due to inbuilt tendencies, i.e., attachments, strong desires, anger, greed, ego, etc. Realising true knowledge and dispelling doubts are essential for experiencing the idea in its true sense. A change in viewpoint through awareness of gross reality is necessary for peace.

Why do you need skill to perform actions?

We define jobs as skilled and unskilled, but even unskilled jobs require know-how, which might not be taught in schools or books but is mere common sense. Like if a door is opened from hinges instead of a door knob, it requires many times more effort. The right skill not only enables us to perform any task but, in every walk of life, saves us from unnecessary labour and is of utmost importance for safety. Imagine a person driving a state-of-the art car without knowing how to drive. It can be disastrous not only for the driver but for others too.

Stress and emotional pain are also hazards; they are slow poison. The human brain, though it is sharp and a storehouse of intelligence, can be damaging unless trained correctly on how to stay calm using higher skills. Emotions inflict more pain than physical agony.

Action is unavoidable for all living beings. Action is not limited to professions to earn money but also responses to melodrama around everyone. And hence failure and success. Actions are associated with anxiety, worry, and fear. Stress

Kills! It is known to be the foremost cause of burnout and health issues. Negativity instils fear and carries away wisdom, which clouds decision making. One can't be sure whether his thoughts at a particular moment are negative or realistic. There are many ways to act in a situation, and selecting the best course of action is difficult. Arjun was also embroiled in confusion about the moral obligations of his actions. Numerous factors fill the mind with noise and impair decision-making ability due to clutter. Often, decisions are taken on impulse. Even knowing that something is wrong, man continues to do it under the influence of emotions, which he later repents of, sometimes throughout life. In the same way, in spite of knowing the consequences, obsessions also drive men to take decisions that lead to disaster.

Yoga is hence the skill to keep miseries of life at bay and improve productivity. It is a method to retain joy amidst the inevitable challenges of daily life. Once one masters this technique of remaining unaffected in all circumstances, he realises that he already possesses what he has been seeking through various efforts and means. It is the key to internal joy and eternal bliss! This is not the pretence of being happy, but *Sthithpragya* state (explained later). It is the actual good feeling that lit up the same world, which otherwise looked like pain.

Yoga is also not a dull, boring, or stale lifestyle. Whereas it is key to stress-free work. It is the ultimate technique to be happy without any dependence on outside factors—the discovery of natural happiness. The portrayal of Sri Krishan as always cheerful, simple, and sweet directs us towards the correct path of yoga, but it demands consistent practice, perseverance, determination, and enthusiasm. Yogi is not the one who performs difficult spiritual or occult practices, but the one who remains equipoised. This is an essential first understanding to upgrade life and follow the Bhagavad Gita in day-to-day life.

The vow is to keep checking. Am I relaxed and unperturbed? Am I free of fear and anxiety? Nothing should be able to disturb this natural state of mind amidst the chaos and uncertainty of life. Maintaining resolute determination is crucial to staying steadfast and unruffled in the face of external circumstances and avoiding impulsive reactions. This is the repetitive practice of applying the right knowledge at each moment.

In the words of Dr. Dean Ornish - *'stress is the information.'* Stress is a sign that your lower instincts have taken over and are controlling you.

> ***Yoga doesn't make life dull but restores natural happiness within***

4.

STEPS FOR THE PRACTICE OF YOGA

How to remain equipoise amidst the melodrama of life? Not that only good things will happen if one follows the path of yoga. Humans are emotional beings, which sets them apart from machines or robots. He has likes and dislikes. He possesses an ego.

Equanimity can't be forced. It can't be pretended. It is not the way to behave. It is not a composed demeanour. Equanimity is the outcome of the philosophy of life. It is a change in the way to think and live. Arjun's doubts and Sri Krishan's explanations in the Gita have remained relevant for thousands of years because these are true laws of nature. In easy terms, these are like scientific laws, similar to Newton's gravitational force, the Archimedes principle, etc.

Understanding life's principles and human nature is essential to attain and sustain equanimity for happiness. To rise above the ordinary and mediocre way to look at the world and everything around it.

Sri Krishan's task is difficult. He is to convince the most ferocious warrior and an intellectual person. His assignment is not only to motivate and overcome the fear of consequences but also to provide moral justification for the war against cousins to get back the kingdom, requiring the killing of grandfather, teachers, many other kings, and thousands of other innocent people. Sri Krishan is not a parent or master who can order, "Do as I say." He is not a corporate boss who can lure staff with nice postings, increments, promotions, or appraisals. He is a mere friend. One is always free to argue with a friend, disagree with him, or even mock him. The job is also more difficult, as Sri Krishan represents divinity. So whatever he says matters. It has to be the truth, not just to hoodwink anybody with pep talk to serve this purpose or achieve goals.

The foremost step towards following yoga is to possess the right knowledge. The natural outcome of true knowledge is dispassion towards worldly matters or detachment, which, in the most apt way, is defined as *Vairagya*. Skilful and right action with *Vairagya* leads to *karma-yoga*. Practicing karma-yoga leads to gaining divine wisdom, fostering devotion, and ultimately achieving liberation.

We will explore these concepts further …..

Steps to the practice of Yoga

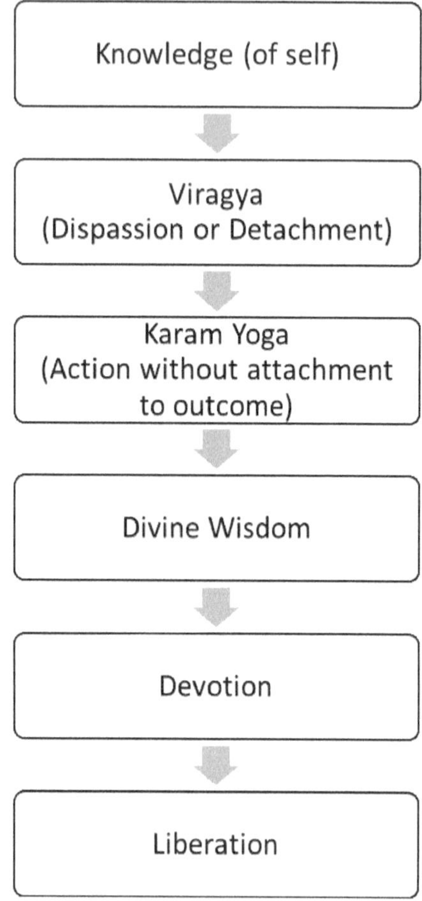

5.

SELF-AWARENESS

In the dark, jet-black night, a thunderstorm was tearing the vast sea apart, spreading everywhere, even to the farthest place one could see. Still, two gunshots from the boat pierced through the deafening sound, and the furious waves threw him into the never-ending sea from the boat, which exploded the very next moment. Though in pain from bullets in his back and hips, he smiled because he knew that he had won, but soon he lost consciousness. By chance, a fisherman on another boat came to throw the trash, spotted a man floating on the debris in the pitch-dark ocean, and, with the help of his friends, rescued him. The doctor in the boat removed the bullets from his body. As he gained consciousness, he attacked fishermen, but he was too weak to fight. He reluctantly accepted fishermen as friends but couldn't answer their question, "Who are you?"

He suffered from amnesia. Desperate and frustrated in such a situation! He later adopted the name Jason Charles Bourne, as he felt it was probably his name, but kept pursuing the search for identity throughout the movie based on one of the most adventurous spy novels of 1980 by Robert Ludlum – Bourne's identity.

Aren't we all in the same situation? We get thrown into this world without any identity, with nearly no thinking ability, and become dependent on strangers taking care of us, who become parents. We accept the names given to us by our parents as our identity. Not only does the world know us by this name, but we also identify ourselves with it. Hardly a few of us get bothered to find more of ourselves. But wise and enlightened seekers contemplate this issue extensively. Jason Bourne kept trying to find the real name and whereabouts he had before he met with an accident. But spiritual aspirants have been searching to know more about their journey before birth as well as after death.

One such government official, M. Sivaprakasam Pillai, went to the Virupaksa cave in Arunachala Hill and met Sri Ramana Maharshi in 1902. The saint hardly spoke to anyone, so Sivaprakasam wrote the question on the sand, *Nan Yar* (who am I?). The answer of the learned sage and his other teachings got compiled in the famous book in 1905 - Who am I? This book has awakened numerous spiritual aspirants. The book is considered a classic in the realm of spiritual literature.

The composition of a six-stanza poem by Adi Shankaracharya, famous as *Atamshatkam* or *Nirvanashatkam*, beautifully attended to the same query, giving the gist of Vedantic teachings. Self-awareness is the first step towards wisdom. It is the foundation pillar on which the rest of life is based.

Self-inquiry, asking 'Who am I?', leads to a silent revolution within a seeker.

"Am I immortal?"

"Am I body or mind?"

"The soul is not born or dies. It is unborn, eternal, everlasting, and primaeval. Even when the body is slain, the soul is not."

(BG 2.20)

The soul only changes the body. The body, after birth, passes through various stages and finally ends with death. Uncountable numbers of men have been on this earth earlier, and uncountable numbers will come in the future. Earth is not the only planet in this universe. No one knows how many universes are co-existing. Man is not the only creation of God. God of men, animals, birds, reptiles, insects, etc., everything is the same. All beings are created by the same universal energy, and we call him God. I am no exception. There is no reason why I deserve better. I am also subjected to the same law of karma, which drives everyone.

Although it is a predominant belief in Hinduism that the soul is imperishable and eternal, Sri Krishan gives another argument to Arjun, saying that even if you believe that the soul is subject to birth and death, there is nothing to grieve. The death of all who have been born is inevitable. Wisdom lies in the realisation that nothing is permanent, so why attach so much importance to events or things or even be possessed by attachments to any person or possession?

Everything here is temporary. Man believes himself to be this body, whereas the body perishes. He believes he is intelligent, but his mind is also the creation of nature. He forgets that he is not immortal but continues to engage in worldly matters, as if he will live forever. The individual gets overpowered by his desires and senses. He ignores the flavour of inner joy. Due to the limitations of the human mind, or, say, Maya, one attaches so much importance to oneself and one's life.

Sri Krishan just reminded Arjun of reality. He didn't invent this concept or reveal it for the first time. This is the eternal knowledge of the Vedas and the Upanishads. The description of self or soul described as part of Sankhya philosophy in chapter 2 of the Gita is the guiding force. It helps to give up attachments, ego, and other negative virtues to progress on the path of tranquillity. Self-awareness brings clarity to the fact that I am not what I have believed so far. So much self-pride or guilt is a waste. I am just part of this creation, like everyone around me. And this uncovers the hidden divinity within everyone and everything.

AtmaShatkam

(Originally composed by Sri Adi Shankaracharya in
Sanskrit.)

I am not mind, intelligence, ego, or memory.
Neither hearing (ears) nor tasting (tongue), smelling (nose), or
seeing (eyes).
Neither sky nor earth nor fire nor air.
The form of blissful consciousness: I am Shiva, I am Shiva.

Neither vital energy (prana) nor the five types of breath,
Neither the seven-material essence (dhatu) nor the five sheaths (of
the body).
Neither speech, hand, feet, nor organs of excretion.
The form of blissful consciousness: I am Shiva, I am Shiva.

Neither I hate nor attachment, nor do I have greed, infatuation,
Neither pride nor haughtiness nor feelings of envy or jealousy.
Neither dharma (righteousness), artha (wealth), kama (desire),
nor moksha (liberation).
The form of blissful consciousness: I am Shiva, I am Shiva.

Neither virtue nor sin, neither pleasure nor sorrow,
Neither sacred hymns nor sacred places, neither sacred scriptures
nor scarifies.
I am neither experience, nor experienced, nor the experiencer.
The form of blissful consciousness: I am Shiva, I am Shiva.

Neither I fear death nor the distinction of caste,
Neither do I have a father and mother, nor do I have birth.
Neither relatives nor friends, neither spiritual teacher nor disciple,
The form of blissful consciousness: I am Shiva, I am Shiva.

I am devoid of duality and formless form,
I am present everywhere, pervading all senses.
I am neither attached to anything nor freed or captive.
The form of blissful consciousness: I am Shiva, I am Shiva.

6.

SPELL OF IGNORANCE

The Sanskrit word *Avidya* implies ignorance. It is the opposite of *Vidya,* which means knowledge. Ignorance leads to misconceptions and is therefore considered the primary cause of all misery. Humans are blessed with the best intelligence among all creatures, but their intelligence is not developed to the level that enables them to perceive the reality of the cosmos and this world.

In this context, Patanjali further defines 'ignorance' as seeing the temporary, impure, and painful as eternal, pure, and pleasant. In crude terms, wrong as right and false as truth.

It is common to observe a moth or insect repeatedly hitting a window in an attempt to escape. It can see the world or light on the other side, but it fails to understand why he is unable to go through glass. Even if there may be an open space or clear passage a few metres from the glass, the insect fails to make its way until, by chance, after repeated attempts, he reaches that spot. Insects have limited minds, as we all know. So do we, but we don't realise it.

"The appearance of the world is a confusion, as even the blue colour of the sky is an optical illusion," says Sage Valmiki in the Yoga Vasishta.

Maya

One fine morning, disciples of Chuang Tzu, a renowned Chinese philosopher, found him a little puzzled. They questioned the master about the cause of his confusion. Chuang Tzu told them that last night he dreamt that he was a butterfly flying around from flower to flower, enjoying the fresh air and soothing sunlight in a lovely garden in King's palace. He felt free and liberated. But then something happened, and he got up. Now he was puzzled as to whether Chuang Tzu was dreaming that he was a butterfly or if this butterfly was dreaming that it was Chuang Tzu.

In another similar story, one afternoon Janaka, the ruler of grand city Videha, after a meal, while on his throne in the courtroom, surrounded by his ministers and brave army chiefs, dozed off after lunch. He dreamt that another king with a large army had invaded his country and was on the verge of entering his palace. In no time, an army of the enemy entered the palace and then the courtroom and started slaying his soldiers and ministers. He somehow managed to escape from the palace on a horse with the help of his loyalists, who also got killed. Alone, he entered the forest to protect himself from chasing enemy soldiers. After a while, he felt safe, but then he realised that he had entered a foreign territory that was also hostile towards his kingdom. He left his horse on the outskirts of the city and took off his ornaments to look like an ordinary person. Exhausted by now, he began to feel hungry and thirsty. He was wounded, barefooted, and in tattered clothes. He saw a rich man distributing food to the beggars. In desperation, he joined the queue, but by the time it was his turn, no more food was left. He dragged himself to the place where food was being cooked and pleaded for something to eat. Taking pity on his condition, someone gave him a handful of rice scraped from the bottom of the vessel on a leaf plate. He was filled with intense joy, as if he had gained a treasure. He sat down in a corner to eat the food, then all of a sudden, two raging bulls came to the place fighting, and in the melee, Janaka's bowl got broken into pieces and food got spilled on the ground. A nearby dog rushed towards the food on the ground. While Janaka tried to take food from the dog, it bit him. Janaka cried with pain. The dignitaries around him got alarmed to see the state of the king; they could also hear the faint scream coming out of the king's mouth.

Janak woke up traumatised! And at that very moment, the scenario changed. He realised that he was safe among his family, friends, and members of the court, amidst all the luxuries and opulence.

He was perplexed by the question - What is real? This or that?

He put that question to all the scholars in the kingdom, but no one could satisfy him. Then the legendary saint Ashtavakra entered his court and whispered into the ear of Janaka, "Neither this nor that is real." Raja Janaka at once became joyful. His confusion got sorted out. The Ashtavakra Gita is another remarkable book in Hindu philosophy for seekers, giving a detailed account of the dialogue between Ashtavakra and Janak.

Maya - Deception is an important dimension in Hindu philosophy, which says that the world is unreal but man, due to his limited understanding, remains engulfed in his own wrong notions. The human mind continues to develop and expand as individuals age. A child starts to grasp matters with age, which he failed to understand in his early years. Birds and animals, too, have intelligence, but it does not develop to the level of humans. In the same way, the human mind never matures enough to understand the reality behind this universe. Although man has made a lot of progress in science, his mind still operates according to the guidelines set forth in the software that nature created.

Man, bewildered by ignorance, continues to look for comfort at the wrong places in the wrong things and remains deprived of what is always with him—natural bliss. This is *Maya*, the trap.

Maya is also termed ignorance, but another school of thought further differentiates both with the belief that Maya emanates from God, whereas ignorance is associated with living beings. Maya is divine.

Vivek Chudamani verses 109 to 116 explain *Maya*, with the disclaimer that *Maya* can't be described in words. *Kshepa* Shakti and *Avritti* Shakti are two types of influences that further explain the concept of Maya.

Rajas (explained later) possess *Vikshepa Shakti* – power to project. It is the origin of all activities. This creates mental modifications such as attachment, grief, etc. It is the cause of lust (Kama), anger, greed, hypocrisy, arrogance, jealousy, egoism, and envy, which causes bondage.

Avritti is veil – It is the power of *Tamas*, which hides reality, and as a result, things appear different from what they are. This power is the origin of the action of *Vikshepa* Shakti (the projection power) of *Maya*. Ignorance, laziness, dullness, sleep, indulgence, stupidity, etc. are attributes of *Tamas*. Due to this, men fail to comprehend reality.

Under the influence of these two veiling and projection powers, there is an absence of correct judgement, wrong beliefs, and doubts, which cause misery.

Ego

I am better than others! I deserve more! I am special! The thoughts driven by ego keep troubling men, provoking them to expect more.

Why are we frightened of being nothing?
Can you face the fact that you are absolutely nothing?

Jiddu Krishnamurthi

Patanjali defines ego as the **identity** of consciousness with that which **merely reflects** consciousness (Patanjali vs. 2.6). In terms of deeper spiritualism, it is a wrong understanding due to ignorance when one identifies the soul with that of the instrument of seeing, i.e., mind and body.

Shankaracharya, in verse 298 of his benchmark book, *Vivekachudamani*, defines:

"There are other obstacles also to man, which are causes of samsara*; among these, ego is the root cause and the first distortion."

(*Samsara: repeated cycle of birth, existence, and death)

Ego is also called *duratma*, the wicked. It makes men believe that I am the doer (*Karta*) and an experiencer (*Bhokta*). The false notion imposes various sorrows, sufferings, and imperfections. Individuals often take pride in attributes such as their body, strength, intelligence, and wealth positions, despite having minimal control over these external factors.

Ego builds emotional pressure, which is detrimental to inner peace. Ego not only impacts mental well-being but also serves as a significant contributor to various health issues, such as stress-related ailments and psychosomatic conditions. The need for self-appreciation, glorification, and to get noticed engages people in the 'Activity Trap'. It is the ego, which is the root cause of many conflicts and interpersonal issues, which results in anger and steals away natural bliss.

Am I the doer?

"All actions are being performed by the mode of nature. The fool deluded by ego thinks, "I am the doer." (BG 3:27)

A man bewildered by Maya takes pride in his achievements or feels guilty for his failures.

Can he alone influence outcomes?

In this uncertain world, how can success or failure be only due to one's own efforts or intelligence? Have we not seen an unprecedented turn of events that changed fortunes overnight?

Undoubtedly, success is closely tied to efforts, skills, energy, and strategy. However, outcomes are based on a mix of controllable and uncontrollable factors. Family and place of birth are uncontrollable factors that have a big impact on how people live their lives. Opportunities available in his environment are among numerous other factors influencing life. Actions are limited to controllable factors. Pride while performing actions is due to a misconception. After all, who has made this mind, which generates ideas and creates skills, and this body, which performs or executes these plans?

Know that it is the hidden factor, EGO, that makes us believe that 'it's me'. Everything in this universe is part of the divine. All pleasures are blessings bestowed by the respective demigods or God when pleased with the karma. Due to ignorance, man takes pride in his intelligence, strength, and energy, despite the fact that his mind and body are not his creation but rather a temporary gift from the divine.

7.

A MAN OF STABLE WISDOM

Sthithpragya is a mixture of two words – *Sthith* means stable (fixed), and *Pragya* implies wisdom. A man whose intelligence is established in stable wisdom.

Arjun asks, "What are the traits of the man who attains *the Sthithpragya* state of mind?" Sri Krishan defines:

"When man casts off all the Kamana (cravings) of the mind and is satisfied in self, through self then he is called Sthithpragya. One who is not disturbed (in mind) even amidst miseries, or who is elated when there is happiness, and who is free from passions (raag), fear, and anger, is called a sage of steady mind. One who is without any affection or attachment to everything and whatever good or evil he may obtain, neither praising it nor despising it, is firmly fixed in perfect knowledge.

One who is able to withdraw his senses from sense objects, as the tortoise draws its limbs within the shell, is firmly fixed in perfect consciousness." (BG 2.55 to 2:58)

The *Sthithpragya* state of mind is the goal of every aspirant on the path of yoga. But the man has a forgetful memory. Due to built-in software, he becomes overwhelmed by emotions. Beside other aspects, equanimity is also akin to the modern concept of emotional intelligence, which is considered today one of the most important and essential traits for leadership and a sign of maturity. Emotional intelligence is the stability of the mind to organise emotions and understand the emotions of people around you to resolve conflicts and have successful interpersonal interactions to optimise decision-making ability. Emotional stability saves grave mistakes caused by impulsive actions and spontaneous outbursts. Emotional intelligence is more of a behavioural aspect, whereas equanimity in yoga is the outcome of an overall attitude developed through awareness in addition to behavioural maturity.

It is not something one can switch on like a fan or, once mastered, stay forever, but a lifelong practice.

8.

TRAP OF DESIRES AND SENSES

Yayati was a great Indian king, with unmatchable wealth and power. He was blessed with a large, loving family and enjoyed all the happiness in the world. Once, he annoyed a sage by breaking his promise. The sage cursed him, saying that he would lose his youth and grow old.

Yatati pleaded with the sage to take back his curse. At last, the sage pacified and said, "Even the gods find it hard to follow the path of virtue when confronted with desires. Being a mortal, it was perhaps more difficult for you to stay on the righteous path. But my curse cannot be undone. If any one of your sons would give up his youth in exchange for your old age, you can be young again."

The king had some respite. His family loved him, and he had many sons. He called all his sons and told them about the curse as well as the way out. He was sure all his sons would volunteer to take his curse on them to rescue him, but no one came forward, which made him very sad. After all, grown up sons refused to give up their youth. The youngest son, Puru, stepped forward and volunteered to take old age to get him back to youth.

Yayati looked at him with an open mouth and said, "You are so young, barely out of teenage. You have so much to see in this world."

All the other sons, who felt the father was unreasonable in asking them to give up their youth to stay young, had the same question.

Puru smiled and said, "Our father has been enjoying all the pleasures of this world for years, and still, he is unsatisfied. What difference will it make whether I get old now or after many decades? I am also bound to remain dissatisfied till death. We all owe so much to our father. We still want to stay young, as we feel we will continue to enjoy it forever or until satisfaction comes to us. Desire is like fire. It can never be quenched. It only grows stronger each time one appeases it by indulging in it. This is a trap."

That was a moment of awakening for Yayati. The great truth dawned on him. He accepted destiny. He gave his kingdom to the wise son Puru and lived like an ascetic for the rest of his life.

Desires and senses

What causes us to become so attached to outcomes? Why is it difficult for us to simply let go? It is because of a simple reason that all actions originate from some sort of desire.

Therefore, it is natural to have expectations for a positive outcome, which leads to anxiety or fear. Desire is the primary motivator for initiating any action. However, desires persist throughout life without ever reaching satisfaction. It is a natural process and can't be stopped. This creates a vicious cycle of perpetual work in pursuit of fulfilling desires. Those seeking enjoyment through indulging in mental cravings will find themselves continuously dissatisfied, as one desire is swiftly replaced by another. Efforts to satisfy cravings are a never-ending race.

Desires are not necessarily evil; many of them are necessities for survival today or beyond. But the meaningless desires, which are not aligned with the goals or real requirements, consume vital life energy and time.

Another more dangerous characteristic of strong desire, i.e., lust, is that it clouds wisdom. Lust is not limited to just cravings of the senses but can take various forms. But the lust or urge of sense is so strong that it weakens the ability to discriminate between right and wrong by distorting the view. Humans often forsake their true goals and pursue illusions, seeking satisfaction and joy through the fulfilment of desires. That is why Sri Krishan cautions Arjun to know lust (*Kamana*) as the most formidable enemy of man and to kill it. (*BG 2.43*)

When Arjun asks why people commit sin, Sri Krishan explains:

"It is lust (intense desires), which appears as wrath. It is insatiable and grossly wicked. Know this as an enemy. As fire is covered by smoke, the mirror by dust, and the embryo by the womb, so is

knowledge covered by desire. Knowledge is covered by this eternal enemy of the wise in the form of lust, which is an insatiable fire.
The senses, the mind, and the understanding are seats of lust; screening the truth through these, lust deludes the embodied soul."

(B.G. 3:37 to 3:40)

Just as light changes colour when passing through a filter, lust affects individuals through their senses, thoughts, and understanding.

But if one were to completely eliminate all cravings and live without desires, what would be left? Without pleasures, what will life be like?

The pleasures of the senses are not only limited to touch, which primarily implies sex, but also include the other four senses: tasty food, nice music, pleasant smell, appreciating scenic beauty, nature, aesthetics, etc., which are not seen as objectionable.

How can one practice this approach while still alive and engaged in daily life? If forced, these virtues become punishment.

The solution lies not in complete abstinence from sensory pleasures but in practicing restraint and moderation. The overall objective is not to let senses create attachments that overpower discrimination. The awareness that clinging to senses is waste, as factors outside give pleasure, but these are short lived and require a regular supply of more and more fuel, is the foremost step. Practicing self-restraint is the key to experiencing lasting inner joy and happiness.

The remedy to pacify an incessant urge or craving is the feeling of *tripti* (satisfaction), which is the key to the kingdom of peace. And satisfaction comes through knowledge of self. Self restraint, being satisfied, and having gratitude for what there is are tools to overcome the strong, intoxicating influence of sense and lust.

With knowledge and practice, one can refuse to be a puppet of these natural instincts and find rest through the technique of yoga. Actions that are not influenced by intense desires (lust or *kamana*) are guided by intelligence.

Desires and senses can cloud your judgement and ability to make wise choices, leading you away from your true path and into the illusion of temporary pleasure that ultimately results in suffering.

He who can withstand here in the body the urge of lust and anger is the Yogi and the happy man. (BG 5.23).

Inner joy rests on the foundation of self–restraint and satisfaction developed through knowledge.

Unless there is discipline of mind and senses, there can't be discrimination, and hence peace.

While pursuing achievements and pleasures, one may discover that true and lasting satisfaction always remains elusive, leading to a continuous quest for fulfilment. One has to contain his expectations or desires to experience inner joy. The relentless pursuit of material possessions and wealth is endless and ultimately detrimental to lasting happiness.

9.

ROUTE TO JOY - VAIRAGYA

"Knowledge is better than practice (without understanding); meditation is superior to knowledge; and renunciation to the fruits of action is even superior to meditation. Peace immediately follows renunciation. (BG 12:12)"

Vairagya, described as renunciation, detachment, or dispassion, is essential for progress on the path of yoga.

Vairagya is a complex concept to understand and difficult to follow. People leave houses, change their dresses to robes, and declare to the world that they are no longer in the materialist race; they give up families to live in religious places. But soon get overpowered by the basic nature to get involved in the same mundane stuff like favouritism, likes and dislikes, position, role, self-importance, and sometimes even immoral practices, while performing the chores in religious places. After all, these are our instincts, the way we are programmed. At the same time, *Vairagya* is the overall shield, and therefore Sri Krishan emphasises it at every juncture of his dialogue with Arjun in the Bhagavad Gita.

The Yog Vasishtha, another important scripture, which is pre-dated from the Bhagavad Gita and narrates the discussion of Sri Ram with masters Rishi Vishvamitra and Rishi Vasishtha, also stresses *Vairagya*. Rishi Vishwamitra, while confirming the wisdom of Lord Ram in the court of King Dashrath, says:

The definite sign of a man of the highest wisdom is that he is not attracted by the pleasures of the world, and for him, even the subtle tendencies have ceased. When these tendencies are strong, there is bondage; when they have ceased, there is true liberation. He is a liberated sage who, by nature, is not swayed by sense pleasures, the motivation of fame, or any other incentives.

Maharshi Patanjali, at verse 1.15, says that one who gives up thirst for what is seen or heard; his *Vairagya* is called self-mastered.

Human instincts often complicate life by introducing various challenges and conflicts. There are numerous issues to keep men on edge. The only solution to continuous worries and anxiety is *Vairagya*. But this is not natural. Humans develop attachments. The best place to observe how we get overpowered by emotions is to visit a cinema hall. All sensible people, in spite of their complete awareness of how movies are scripted and filmed, cry, laugh, and get thrilled by action scenes, knowing well that these are unreal. We get attached to characters, pray for their welfare, and take a sigh of relief when the scheme of the villain is exposed and bad characters are brought to justice or revenge is successful. The ending of the movie lightens up the mood or keeps us sad even a few hours after the movie. The movie inside the theatre ends in around two hours. But reality is for a much longer duration; it goes on for a complete lifetime, and every individual performs a role in it, which is not carefully written beforehand or filmed using techniques. No retakes! The story is full of suspense, as the future can't be certain. Moreover, there is no next movie to watch, and it can end abruptly without prior notice or keep going when it appears to be ending at any moment. There is no predictability, like in most movies, that in the end, the hero will win and the bad character will lose. In this movie, the individual himself is the hero; he is the best character but can still remain victimised by circumstances till the end. Unlike in the movie inside the theatre, in spite of everything, viewers may not have any sympathy for him.

So why, in real life, will emotions not be so overwhelming?

In an episode in Mahabharat, Yudhishthira faced a lot of questions from a Yaksha. One such question was: What is the most amazing thing in this world? Yudhishthira answered that the most amazing thing is that, though humans are mortal and will die one day, everyone keeps going about their lives as if they are here forever.

However, many times frustration, failure, and the death of loved ones develop *vairagya*. The movement of frustration, failure, and pain gets healed with time, and man gets back to a normal life. Similarly, dispassion born of circumstantial causes or utter disgust is also temporary. Some experiences, like a visit to the cremation ground, the touch of a spiritual master, or reading a nice book, give realisation and hence detachment. But these feelings are short-lived, most of the time, and man returns to the same daily ritual because the pure *vairagya* emerges from awareness of the reality of the world, which unveils the intelligence required for day-to-day practice.

Where Yayati is a reflection of ignorance, his son Puru denotes knowledge, which creates dispassion. Chuang Tzu's dilemma: Whether it is a butterfly or Chuang Tzu, who is dreaming? Raja Janak's dilemma: what is real? This or that life... such questions poke us to contemplate the futility of our possessions, losses, power, fame, worry, etc.

The scriptures say that the world is unreal and that it is desire that creates the world or even many universes. It is a very deep statement. Rishi Vasishtha says to Sri Ram in Yog Vasishtha, "Men remain so busy with diverse affairs in this world, in pursuit of pleasure or power, and do not desire to know the truth, which they obviously don't see."

It is difficult for an ordinary person to comprehend, but it is said that man, at the time of death, starts realising that he has been living in a world that is unreal. On the death bed, when a person comes to know that he will die soon, he realises the worthlessness of all his desires, pursuits, possessions, or even regrets. Sri Krishan also first creates awareness about the soul and the temporary nature of the world to lay the foundation for the concept of *Vairagya* in the Bhagavad Gita.

Is this world unreal? The query from King Janak was answered by Ashtavakra. He whispered in the ear of Raja Janak, "Both are unreal!"

We are trapped in our own minds. Even if everything is temporary, the whirlpool of world affairs is so strong that one remains entangled in it with one or another rationale. At the same time, looking back at the theory of natural bliss, one has no other option but to come out of it. Freedom from sorrow or realization is impossible unless one has a conviction that the word is unreal.

Maya creates a magic spell. Maya is also an illusion of separateness, as it is the same divine energy that is behind everything. Like a mirage that appears to be a real river on a hot afternoon in a desert, this creation appears to be real. Like a poor animal who keeps chasing mirage in the desert in hope of quenching his thirst, we continue to run after objects of desire to find happiness. Since the death of anyone born is inevitable, it is indisputable that the world is temporary. This awareness of the temporary nature of the world and the nature of desires is the foundation of dispassion.

Vairagya emerges from knowledge and discrimination of real and unreal, beyond the influence of Maya. It originates from the self - realisation that I am neither mind nor body but soul. Identity with this body is a misconception, as the body is temporary and the journey of the soul has been continuing from one body to another. The body takes birth and dies after passing through various stages, but the soul is beyond birth and death; it is everlasting, primaeval, imperishable, and eternal and can't be slain.

In addition to the holiness attached to *vairagya, or* detachment, let's examine the practical utility of the concept.

It is said that in Persia, once a mighty king assembled all the wise men in his kingdom and asked them to create something for him that would make him happy when he was sad. All these wise men, after long deliberation, presented the king with a ring inscribed - This too shall pass. The profound phrase reminds us of the impermanence or temporariness of every situation. Since then, the phrase has been echoing in the Jewish as well as the western world.

As mentioned earlier, happiness is not something to look for. A man is born with it. One only gets deprived of it due to *Raag* and *Dwesh* (passions and aversions), which once removed; the mind rests in its natural state. Passions - aversions, attachment to self, and lust, leading to anxiety and fears deprive man of natural bliss. Man wants comfort and happiness. He continues to look for it in various sources. The attachment to the body, feeding senses, and ego is like the dog enjoying the blood oozing out of the gums when it chews the dry bone, causing injury. When *vairagya* starts setting in, the things around us start losing importance, and there is a lack of craving for pleasures. *Vairagya,* in a way, is the best course of action in self interest. It is the comfort we always seek. With this realisation, *vairagya* (dispassion) strengthens and focus shifts to preserve natural bliss from the never-ending melodrama of daily life. As dependence on outside factors reduces, the negative virtues of lust, greed, and, hence, anger and frustration subside, and dispassion grows further. This silent revolution inside changes everything.

Self-obsession is the biggest hidden factor, which never lets dispassion settle. What will happen to me? What do others think of me? These worries, due to self-importance, pride, and the natural instinct to be secure, appreciated, loved, etc., remain hidden under layers of mind and keep the mind engrossed, derailing the practice of *Vairagya*. We keep trying to prove ourselves. We live with the belief that we should have control over everything happening around us. We ignore the fact that we don't know when death will take any one of us in its grip, and the story of life can end abruptly. We don't see far enough to realise the fact that if we live up to old age, we may become dependent on others. Our great minds may lose memory. Moreover, we have been dependent in childhood. Wisdom is in accepting that, including me, no one is an exception here. There is nothing unique about me. We take ourselves so seriously. We care so much about the opinions of people around us who are also mortal, will not be here forever, and have their own desires and imperfections like us. In ignorance, we are living with a fake sense of self-importance when everything belongs to the divine.

Vairagya is just a change in perspective and giving up attachments, not anything else. One still pursues his business, friends, family, etc., but with a sense of dharma rather than normal instincts. *Vairagya* is also not disinterested in action. Yogi also strives to achieve success through efforts, but with knowledge and a sense of duty, which leads to acceptance of any outcome – favourable or unfavourable.

There is lots and lots of self-control, in the practice. All pleasure and pain are felt. 'Letting go' is not as easy as it sounds.

Vairagya is not a final destination but a lifelong path of practice against human instincts. In order to move forward, it is useful to remove some misconceptions about the concept of *vairagya* in yoga.

Demystifying *Vairagya*

Vairagya is certainly not switching over to robes. The traditional impression of *Vairagya* is to embrace hardships and live a secluded, simple, selfless life, which is quite contrary to Sri Krishan. He is known as a lover, charming, jovial, and king. His image is not that of a helpless, fragile, all forgiving man but, on the contrary, carries an unmatchable grandeur. This misconception about *vairagya* is the biggest hindrance to its acceptance by a normal man. It is treated as something very pious and rigorous, and hence a subject of hardcore spiritual enthusiasts.

It certainly does not mean being a sad or serious type of person. It is not just the opposite of the life of a fun seeker. *Vairagya* is not embracing unnecessary hardships; it is actually joy because self-restraint and discipline lead to freedom from self-created bondages. *Vairagya* is an approach to seeing the bigger picture based on knowledge. It is dispassion towards everything in life; giving up attachments with awareness that everything here is transient in nature. Happiness, which I am pursuing through money, fame, appreciation, etc., is an illusion. All these things can't always be mine. Ups and downs are bound to happen. Short-lived happiness creates addiction, and soon I need more doses to have the same or a better feeling of joy. As a result, I have been trapped in a vicious circle throughout life. Once reliance shifts from outside factors to inner joy (Atman Sukh), the world changes. Man, dispassionate towards never ending worldly affairs, is neither agitated by grief nor hankers for pleasures and lives free from lust, fear, and anger. There are no, or just a few, needs. All the restlessness subsides.

Vairagya is also not being indifferent, avoiding hardships, and taking the easy path. Let anything happen to me, my family, my friends, society, or organisation; I need not act because I have adopted the path of *Vairagya* is a gross misunderstanding. Such thoughts are *Tamsik* in nature. It also does not mean to let people take advantage of you. The Gita originates from the dilemma of whether to give up or act, and it is an effort to inspire a friend to take up the challenge wholeheartedly, which he was not emotionally prepared for. He was overwhelmed with the thought of the futility of victory, even though his family rightfully deserved it. Sri Krishan, at this juncture, advises that whatever one has to perform as per the circumstances and duty can't be given up. But working with *Vairagya* implies using discrimination to avoid pursuing ego and attachment to outcomes. It is acceptance of anything that comes up after efforts. It is also working with the knowledge that everything is temporary here, as it is often said in Hindi: *Sab Maya Hai!* Everything is an illusion.

"He who does his duty without expecting the fruit of his actions is a Sannyasi (hermit) and Yogi both. (6:1). "

Death is inevitable, and hence everything is temporary. Why subject oneself to misery due to the natural instinct of the attachment?
We create misery and self-injury by giving so much importance to ourselves and keep trying to prove ourselves to others who are equally imperfect and are temporarily here.
Vairagya is not dull, sad, be serious, or wearing robes. It is acceptance of all types of outcomes.
Detachment is the tool for wise to get out of overwhelmed emotions.
Primarily, vairagya is: awareness to avoid attachments; giving up attachment to fruits of action; knowing the futility of hankering for pleasures; and vanity of Ego – Self-importance.

10.

INSIGHT ON KARMA

Before enlightenment, chop wood and carry water. After enlightenment, chop wood and carry water. – Zen proverb

Self-awareness creates many different inferences. It can be concluded that it is futile to toil for success or pursue goals, as one day everything will go to waste. Or one should only pursue enjoyment and pleasure, as nothing matters here. Action being the central theme, the Bhagavad Gita covers a comprehensive investigation of all aspects of karma (action).

Since birth, all beings have been engaged in something or other, with or without any objective. Activities are also undertaken to keep oneself busy.

Everyone is haplessly driven to action by modes of nature (BG 3.5). Desiring action, one can't even maintain his body (BG 3.8).

The significance of work is better explained with the example that God himself remains engaged in work, though he has no obligations or anything to achieve. Nature can be seen continuously involved in the cycle of evolution, creation, destruction, etc. Science has found that the universe is ever-expanding. Earth and other planets continue to move around the sun in their respective orbits, which creates seasons and, hence, the growth of crops and food.

Work is not only essential for survival, but it is also the identity of a person. It is not limited to a profession. Even those who have sufficient resources remain engaged in some sort of activity, either to expand or maintain their wealth or for social status or enjoyment. The mind jumps from one subject to another.

Action is a must, but it brings complexity to life and discomfort. Man, like other animals, remained engaged in action as per his nature to fulfil his needs for food, shelter, and various other desires. We have inbuilt cravings for pleasure. But unlike other animals, the human brain is also the biggest cause of misery. It remains too attached to everything. Our lives are also burdened by extra needs propelled by our ego, in the form of a sense of achievement, self-pride, social status, etc. There is an insatiable desire to amass wealth, fame, or status. Therefore, we tend to drive ourselves more than other beings.

Another dimension is the uncertainty of the future. No one can be sure of success all the time. But one can ruin his life by worrying about the future; still, one can't ensure everything will go right. Success and failure depend on a lot of uncontrollable or unforeseen factors. So much energy is wasted in endless worry. All beings have to undergo difficult times or can get into odd situations. No one has always won and never failed.

Therefore, Sri Krishan's advice for observing skill in action. The key solution lies in taking action with the wisdom of yoga to alleviate the adverse repercussions of one's actions.

In yoga, actions are performed for *Swadharma* as one's own duty. Hence, it liberates a person from confusion about the selection of a course of action because one has a fairly good idea of what his duty is in a given situation.

Besides defining action with equanimity and treating success and failure alike, another popular message of the Gita is:

Your right is to work, but never to the fruit of action. Neither let the fruits of action be motives, nor let attachment be to inaction.

(BG 2.47)

Sri Krishan says that miserable are those who undertake *sakam karma*, i.e., action for satisfying lust (a strong form of desire). Often, in layman's language, it rhymes in Hindi as *Karm Hi Dharm hai*. (Karma is Dharma). There is no option for a man but to keep doing his part of the work (controllable factors) and accept that he has no right to rewards. A farmer at the time of sowing seeds can't be certain that rain will be good and other factors will remain conducive to crops. Many times, the crop fails, but if he does not sow seed, there can't be any yield at the end of the season.

It is not that any action forms *Karmayoga*. Only actions propelled by one's own duty, as per circumstances or dharma, qualify for *Karmayoga*. Such actions are performed not for ego, unrestrained senses, or passions. Karma fuelled by lust invites misery, and actions with a sense of duty bring fulfilment and bliss.

The spiritual dimension of karma

But why does a man have no right to the fruits of his actions? The Gita theory clarifies that pleasure, pain, success, and failure are divine gifts depending on the various accumulated karma of this as well as past lives. The karma of our current lives will also certainly have consequences in the form of pleasure or pain in the immediate future, later in life, or in the next life. The law of karma is irreversible. This concept is fundamental to the Hindu belief system.

As you sow, so shall you reap. Karma yoga is *sadhana,* i.e., practice to fine-tune oneself. This wisdom is not merely for stress relief but for the holistic improvement of current life as well as the journey beyond. It is a union with the Supreme. This journey begins with faith in the laws of karma, and gradually, with time, one starts experiencing the strength of this concept. In the yoga of Sri Krishan, the work is a way to please God.

"The one who is the source of all beings and by whom the whole universe is pervaded, by worshipping him through the performance of his own work, man can attain him" (BG 18:46).

Work also creates bondage because of attachment to the outcome of action. All actions have some effect in the future, called *Karmabandhan*, which triggers the vicious circle as each action also creates many more actions. This is like a chain reaction. The concept can be explained in clear terms with the example of an apple. One can count the seeds in one apple, but no one can say how many apples each seed will produce. However, the only remedy to get out of *Karamabandhan* is to work without attachment to the fruits as a duty.

"Except for actions performed as Yagya (denoting spiritual sacrifices to please God), men in this world get bound by action. Therefore, perform actions, Arjun, without any attachment." (BG 3.9)

Sri Krishan goes a step further and exposes another depth: even inaction that is not doing work is also an action. Sri Krishan also cautioned against abandoning duty.

"If you refuse war, renouncing your Swadharma, you will lose your honour and incur sin." (BG 2.33).

Contrary to the idea of giving up work and the belief that work is the cause of emotional pressure, Krishna's yoga is incomplete without action. The action in his technique is nourishment for the soul as well as a route for spiritual upliftment.

Butcher's Gita

Nothing has better explained the concept of *Karama Yoga* than the story of a hermit and a butcher, also known as the Vyadh Gita, which is part of Mahabharat.

Once upon a time, there was a young boy, Kaushika. He got dispassionate about worldly activities and developed an intense love for the divine. He left the comforts of home and went to the forest to gain wisdom through spiritual practices.

One day, when he was in deep meditation under a tree, some dry leaves fell on his head. A crow and crane were fighting on a branch of the tree, which disturbed him. The young monk got upset, and as he looked at these birds with an angry glance, to his surprise, they burned into ashes. The monk was shocked and filled with remorse. But suddenly, he realised that he had attained supernatural powers, which meant that he was on the right path. He became more rigorous in his practice.

A few days later, he went to the nearby village to seek food. When he knocked, the house lady opened the door. After greeting him, she asked him to wait. A lot of time passed, but she didn't return. The monk was restless, but he knew that he had to control his anger to avoid any damage to the lady. After some time, the lady appeared, offered food to the monk, and apologised for the delay. The monk thought that, had she known that he possessed such powers, she could have been more respectful to him.

While he was engrossed in his thoughts, the lady said, "I am sorry. I was busy looking after my husband, as he was unwell. By the way, don't worry; I am not like those birds that got burned by your gaze. But please don't be angry, as anger is the worst enemy of man."

The monk was bewildered! Nobody knew about the birds in that dense forest. He apologised to the lady and pleaded with her to tell him how she came to know about the incident in the forest, where no one else was present. What was the spiritual practice she was following so that she could develop such a vision?

Lady said, "Master, I am an ordinary person. I don't know about any spiritual powers or paths, but I was gifted with this vision. I never desired to have this power, and I feel God has been kind to me, as I always consider serving my husband, in-laws, and kids as my utmost duty. I put all my energy into looking after them with sincerity and live in gratitude for whatever I get. This is only worship or a way to please God, I know."

When the monk was not satisfied and he insisted on knowing more, the lady said, "O young monk, though you have studied scriptures, it appears that you have not understood the true essence of dharam. If you are inquisitive, I would suggest you go to Mithila and meet Dharma Vyadh (butcher), who can answer all your queries."

The monk could not control himself. Though the thought of understanding religion from the butcher was awkward, he had to meet him that day itself to put an end to the mystery. He made a hasty exit for Mithila and arrived at the address he got from the lady. A butcher was engaged in selling meat in the local market. The monk felt embarrassed to approach the butcher with his questions. It might be that the lady told him to meet the butcher to get rid of him. What spiritual knowledge could a learned and blessed monk like him seek from a butcher? Before he could make up his mind, the butcher spotted him. He came to him and took him to a lonely place and said, "I understand; it is an odd place for you, but you have to wait till evening to know the secret of birds and that lady with extraordinary vision in the village."

The monk knew he was in the right place. There was no option but to wait. The monk watched the butcher from a distance, engrossed in his work, cutting and selling meat and bargaining with customers.

In the late evening, the butcher finished his work, and the monk quietly followed him to his house in the dark. After welcoming him home and giving him a comfortable seat, the butcher requested the monk to wait for some time. He went inside his home to look after his old parents and feed them. After finishing other household work, he then returned to the monk and requested that he ask his questions.

The monk asked the butcher, "Why are you selling meat, and how could you acquire such spiritual powers in spite of being in such an unholy profession?"

Butcher replied, "I am selling meat for my living, as my family, has been following this profession for the last many generations. This is the way I am able to earn a living for my family and there is nothing inappropriate about it. Though I am selling meat, I am a vegetarian. I don't kill animals myself, but sell the meat of animals already killed by others. The right path and conduct for man are governed by two factors: keeping control of vices and promoting virtues. The most harmful vices are selfishness, anger, vanity, greed, and crookedness. The most useful virtues are those that keep society together. This approach has to be maintained even after attaining perfection. Non-violence and truth are the pillars of religion, through which the best result can be achieved. During conflict in any difficult circumstances, whatever is good for all beings should be done. Be on the path of non-violence, be compassionate towards all beings, be lawful and just in your conduct. The essence of all virtues is the desire to do well for all beings."

Butcher further said, "O monk, you renounced your home and parents, who needed you in their old age, against their wish, to study holy scriptures, which has caused grief to them and hence they have fallen sick. I advise you to go back and serve them. You are a pure soul, and following this path will not have any adverse impact on your spiritual growth."

That was the moment of awakening for the monk! He thanked the butcher for his profound teachings, which helped him realise the truth. After learning the art of spiritual practice, in the form of *swadharma*, he returned to normal life to earn a living and serve his parents as per the norms of society.

The Dilemma of Selfless Work

I remained puzzled by the recommendation in the Gita for selfless work as an ingredient of Krama Yoga. It was not fitting into my circumstances. How can an ordinary man like me do it? I have to earn a living. If I work for the sake of others, then who will feed my family and me? The requirement doesn't end with mere food and shelter. One has to pay for comforts, better facilities, education, etc. for family members. If I become selfless, others will simply take advantage of me. This makes *Karmayoga*, again, the path of only hermits, not for an ordinary household person. Peace at this cost is very expensive. This is highly irresponsible towards my family. Later on, during my research, I realised the distortion in the meaning in the English translation. Most of the translations and commentaries are written by saints dedicating their lives to the welfare of society. Selfless work may be appropriate from their point of view, but it contradicts my value system.

Beyond doubt, selfless work is valuable for spiritual practice. But is charity the only way for *Karmayogi*? Arjun was fighting for the kingdom for his family, which he believed his cousins had taken from them using unfair means. Another objective was to take revenge for the humiliation his wife had suffered. It was not just for the welfare of others or the majority. If the majority were the criteria, more lives on both sides could be saved by averting the war. Calling war off could have helped more people than fighting. Then why did Sri Krishan keep prompting him to go to war? While instigating Arjun in the beginning, Sri Krishan says:

"Die and you will attain heaven; win and you will enjoy the kingdom of earth; therefore, stand up, Arjun, with determination to fight." (BG 2.37)

It is important to understand the concept of *Swadharma* to grasp the subtle concept of *Karmayoga*.

Rather than calling it selfless work, it is *Nishkaam Karamayoga,* another widely used term that is more appropriate to convey the meaning, where *nishkaam* means without lust (intense desires). The Gita, in its original Sanskrit, mentions the word *kamana*, which is closer to meaning intense desire. This is another word that fails to reflect its true meaning in translation. The word *Kamana* gets defined as *Ichha,* or desires, which confuses the followers. Desires propel any action. Not all desires can be given up. On the path of yoga, focus is on lust, cravings, intense desires, and obsessions, which create restlessness and delude man. The word lust is not limited to sexual desire, as often it is used, but to overall intense desires.

On similar lines, the word *Niswarth* in the Gita means 'not selfish'. It is work performed with a sense of duty, not with selfish intent. This action may or may not be selfless or charitable. Though the value of selfless service can't be undermined, action in Gita doesn't essentially mean charitable work.

There is also self-interest in earning a living, making a house for shelter, working for family, and even expanding business. A shopkeeper who sells goods for profit is not selfless but performs his dharma. That is his way to earn a living. However, selling spurious items or cheating others is selfish. It is *Swadharama* that runs the social system.

Dharma

The great Bali fell like a tree after he was hit by the arrow fired by Sri Ram, who was hiding behind the cover of trees.

Sri Ram and Laxman approached Bali, and he looked at them with disbelief.

"You are famous, descended from a noble family, the son of a king, powerful, modest, and morally upright. How could you kill me while I was engaged in a fight with someone else? I have not done anything wrong to you or your family. I live in the forest and eat fruits and leaves. How will you justify this act? Even the use of the meat, skin, and hair of monkeys by humans for any purpose is prohibited. Is your behaviour in line with dharma?" Bali questioned Sri Ram.

Sri Ram justified his action by stating that it was in accordance with dharma because it was his duty to punish him as he had forcefully taken the wife of his younger brother and Sri Ram's friend Sugreev, though she could have been treated as a daughter-in-law. The argument that Sri Ram could have fought war with him was inapplicable in such circumstances because he was a monkey, and it is acceptable for people from warrior clans to hunt for animals.

Dharma is most often misconstrued as religion. Dharma originates from the Sanskrit word '*dhri*', which means to hold, maintain, and preserve. In a way, these are like conduct linked to the cosmic laws.

The definition of dharma varies and depends upon the prevalent social norms, ethical standards, and understanding of right conduct. This calls for careful deliberation and deeper wisdom.

Dharma is not holy scripture but rather the understanding of situations and the use of discrimination to decide the right course of action.

Swadharma

"From the well performed dharma of others, it is better to perform, even devoid of merit, swadharma (one's own dharma). Better is death in swadharma; the dharma of others is fraught with fear."

(BG 3.35)

Swa-dharma is a righteous way of conduct for anybody, encompassing his morals, virtues, duties, etc. Some elements of *swadharma* vary from person to person with professions, stage of life, cultural value, role assigned to him in social order, etc. In a family, a person performs his duty as a son, father, husband, brother, sister, etc. Sri Krishan kept motivating Arjun to fight, as it was his duty as a warrior on the battlefield. But hardly any one of us is in a war zone. Though sometimes circumstances are similar to war only, it is not always. Still, one or another struggle keeps on going. Even for some lucky few, it may be a very peaceful life, but the demand for action never ends. Though *Swadharma* is a spiritual practice, its benefits extend to even materialistic life in the long run, as a focus on *Swadharam* essentially drives man for betterment by avoiding fritting away energy in unlimited distractions.

Aligning actions with one's swadharma is the cornerstone of spiritual practice, guiding individuals towards a fulfilling and purposeful life.

All actions should be performed without any attachment to the fruit of the action.

Do Good: The law of karma is irreversible.

11.

DIVINE WISDOM

"Out of various *yagya* (sacrifices) performed by yogis to seek the blessings of God, *gyan* (knowledge) *yagya* is superior to all," says Sri Krishan in the Bhagavad Gita. Gyan yagya refers to dedicating time and effort to acquire knowledge. This emphasises the crucial role of knowledge for those seeking spiritual enlightenment.

The Gita itself is a book of knowledge to relieve a man stuck in emotional turmoil, gripped by anxiety, and doubtful about the morality of his decision to take up the war. The teachings of the Gita are not limited to stress management or emotional strength. As one delves deeper into the Gita, its teachings progressively encompass a broader spectrum of life's aspects.

Life encompasses multiple dimensions, each of which holds significance. Acquiring 'right knowledge' is essential for making informed decisions that positively influence various aspects of life, such as relationships, careers, health, and personal growth. This selected path then becomes a lifelong practice. The wrong path not only fails to elevate life and keeps one embroiled in misery but also leads to the waste of precious time.

Knowledge and Divine Wisdom

Wisdom is not just information gathered from books or other sources; it is a deep awareness and realisation. It is the moment when the essence of knowledge becomes deeply ingrained in one's life. Wisdom (divine knowledge) is light within, which is a blessing of the divine and the result of purification attained through the practice of yoga. Divine knowledge reveals hidden truths, fosters profound peace, and elevates individuals to a higher level of understanding beyond ordinary limits. Knowledge, in a way, is just information.

"Without doubt, there is no purifier as great as knowledge. This knowledge is attained within; through the practice of yoga over time. He who has mastered his senses and is devoted to this practice with faith attains wisdom. Upon attaining wisdom, individuals gain clarity on fundamental truths and experience a profound sense of inner peace that transcends external circumstances." (BG 4:38 & 4:39)

As symbolically illustrated in the story of the butcher and saint, the practice of Krama Yoga leads to the release of spiritual powers and the awakening of dormant wisdom.

12.

DEVOTION (BHAKTI)

The Bhagavad Gita consists of eighteen chapters, which can be divided into three sets of six chapters each. The first six chapters are about the nature of the self and elements of yoga involving karma and knowledge. The following six chapters focus on devotion (Bhakti) and the glory of God. The third group focuses on an intellectual discussion about philosophical concepts.

Devotion strengthens with realisation through divine knowledge. Divine love, devotion, or surrender to the will of God, termed Bhakti Yoga, is a significant element of yoga. It is an intense connection between devotee and supreme.

"Certainly, the divine Maya of mine, consisting of modes of nature (guns), is hard to overcome. But those who take refuge in me alone shall cross over this Maya." (BG 7.14)

Devotion is considered the only way to get out of the spell of disillusion caused by the nature and limitations of the human mind to comprehend it.

When we see a larger picture coming out of the periphery of one's religion and set of beliefs about God, there is a common understanding about a universal energy, which is the cause of not only our earth but also the whole universe and life. We have named this supreme divine behind everything in this universe—God, with different names in different parts of the world, languages, and religions. Everything here dwells in God. He is the creator, the preserver, and the destroyer. Throughout history, people have found different ways to worship God. Bhakti yoga is not confined to only the gods of Hinduism. Any other religious practice with devotion can also be defined as Bhakti Yoga because it establishes a connection with divinity.

Is devotion just superstition?

The power of devotion has been realised across the world and religions. Devotees since ages in different parts of the world, which were not even connected or communicating with each other, have experienced and believe in it. While devotion is highly regarded, many religious institutions are also rife with corruption and unethical behaviour. Many of these religious organisations appear to be like any other business. Still, thousands of followers throng around them.

They find bliss in it. They vow to ensure the authenticity of these institutions.

If it has been established that one gets whatever one asks God, then with centuries of experience, everyone could have been religious by now. Only an insane person today could have not been religious. But we know that we don't get everything we ask from God. Is there anyone listening on the other end? It is a complex question. Only those who have practised faith for a long time can answer whether the religion is of any use or just another illusion. Karl Marks said religion is the opium of people. Is this true? Then why do so many find long-lasting peace and nectar in devotion, which is not feasible in anything superfluous or artificial? Do people adopt religion because they are afraid of death and difficulties? Because there are many things beyond control!

Devotion is the technique *(yukti)* of establishing instant connection *(yog)* with the ultimate supreme power, which is so peaceful and blissful. Devotees find immediate bliss in devotion. Surrender of worries, pride, guilt, etc. relieves man of emotional burden and hence the easiest way to peace. We find this connection through any faith. That is why so many religions are successful.

Sri Krishan clarifies in chapter 7, "*With various desires and diverse rituals due to their nature, any devotee seeks to worship with faith, in whatever form, I (Supreme God) make his faith unwavering, and he attains his desires, which in reality are granted by me only.*" It is ultimately the purity of prayer or surrender to the divine that has immense potential, irrespective of faith and religion."

The story of Dhanna Jat, a naïve farmer, is the most apt example of the power of devotion. Dhanna poked a local priest to introduce him to God so that he could live a comfortable life. The priest gave a random stone to Dhana to worship. Surprisingly, Dhanna attained God in that very stone through his wholehearted devotion, which the priest couldn't get through years of spiritual practice.

Sri Krishan categorises devotees into four categories:

- Seeker of worldly possessions
- A man in distress, seeking relief
- Seeker of knowledge
- A man of wisdom

The Gita says that though God fills the desires of all those who worship him, the wise are most dear to him, and such devotees attain the ultimate through practice.

Another reason bhakti is popular worldwide and in various religions is because devotion helps individuals overcome their innate impulses. Devotion and acceptance that God is behind everything around cultivate love and compassion, which makes one feel good. Only with surrender can one keep aside his ego, negative thoughts, fear, etc. As a result, wisdom automatically draws upon him. The connection to the divine source of energy clears thought processes and creates positive vibes, which make people in their surroundings contribute favourably. This mere connection is the unparalleled solace for the soul inside all beings. Bhakti is an essential step in yoga and leads to liberation. When practised with determination and faith, its experience is beyond words.

Distortion in religious institutions

Devotion is not only confined to gods or demigods but can also be towards a holy man or guru. However, sometimes greedy people, due to their oratory or leadership skills, manage to create impressions of holy men. They get prominent positions in religious organisations. Occasionally, even genuine holy men fall prey to their senses or desires after years of self-restraint and get involved in unacceptable, immoral, and even illegal activities. In such cases, devotees feel bewildered and cheated. Humans are inherently imperfect in their actions and behaviours. A master or guru only propagates the eternal knowledge of ancient Vedas, Upanishads, or other scriptures in their way. Even the knowledge of the Gita is the essence of such knowledge. Devotees should know that it is ultimately their spiritual practice, prayer, or connection to the supreme divine that produces results. The true learned master only helps in developing a correct understanding of this knowledge, and thereafter, a devotee is on his own personal journey. The fall of holy men, however, should be seen as a warning sign that when such renowned and elevated men can get entangled in *maya* and yield to sense pleasures and desires, one must remain cautious and exercise discrimination. True devotion also helps in getting over such demonic tendencies. One can deceive others, but not oneself. Superfluous or pretentious conduct may attract some crowds, but it doesn't help in the spiritual journey.

Another challenge posed by religious institutions is the wrong interpretation of the preaching of holy men and scriptures, resulting in encouraging superstitions or creating enmity among faiths. Hostility among people based on faith is primarily political and aims to establish the superiority of one path over another. People of different faiths are all creations of the same divine entity. It is just different names given to the supreme power by men of different religions. The God of men is the same for animals, who don't follow any faith or religion. It is like the race to sell, or sometimes even force, a consumer product to customers. These individuals who claim religious authority are often more concerned with others following their teachings for personal gain than prioritising their own spiritual growth. The spiritual journey is internal, and any approach devoid of love and compassion towards all beings is not only ignorance but also counterproductive. Those involved in such propaganda deprive themselves of divine blessings and their benefits.

Mukti (Liberation)

"Getting rid of passions, cravings, fear, and anger, wholly absorbed in me, depending upon me, and purified by the penance of wisdom, many have become one with me in the past (BG 4:10)."

"Fix your mind to me, be devoted to me, worship me, and bow to me. Having thus linked yourself to me and entirely depending on me, you shall come to me." (BG 9:34)

Since our objective here is to understand the principles of yoga for peace and fulfilment, the interpretation of Sri Krishan as God is left to individual preference and beliefs. (However, Krishan represents the divine throughout the epic book—the Mahabharata, and the Gita is only a small part of it.)

Liberation is the most sought-after ultimate aim of Hindu spiritualism, but the definition of liberation defined as 'Mukti' has many connotations. It is the end of the cycle of birth and death, which ordinary materialist men find difficult to comprehend. The practice of yoga culminates in union with God and liberation from the continuous cycle of birth and death. This may appear too deep for a normal person. Liberation is considered the path adopted by saints living in ashrams and mountains, dedicated to spiritual practice. Liberation as the final goal gives people the strength to follow the discipline of yoga, get over their instincts, and surrender in difficult moments without seeking materialistic rewards from their spiritual practice. It is like an anchor to hold the boat to the shore in storms. Yogi moves through the whirlpool of this world and practices the instructions of yoga against the built-in human tendencies, to reach the final destination of their spiritual practice - *Mukti.*

Gita is the holistic way to live. It is not just a tool for stress management or productivity, though these are its by-products. The search for peace remains elusive unless goals are set right at an early stage after opting for the philosophy of yoga for life.

Without getting into the complexity of the afterlife journey, another more acceptable interpretation of liberation for seekers is freedom in this life. The end of suffering or dependence on the outside world. Liberation from the negative impact in the form of frustration, compulsions, anxiety, fear, anger, etc. is more relevant to materialist men like me. It is pure joy without any reason. This is the immediate benefit of following the steps of Sri Krishan's Yoga: Self-awareness, knowledge, dispassion, wisdom, *swadharma* without attachment to fruits, devotion, which lead to freedom from unnecessary self-created bondages.

Devotion is:

- Acceptance of the reality of supreme energy, which has created my body and mind besides everything around me.
- Praying with or without rituals, etc., or in any other way to connect to the divine.
- Surrendering all success, failure, pleasures, and miseries to the will of God, every moment through practice.
- Seeing God in all beings and accordingly treating them with respect, compassion, and love.

13.

KARMA YOGA OF SQUIRREL

A little-known story of Shri Ram and Squirrel gained popularity when a fifteen-foot-tall metallic sculpture of a squirrel was erected at the Ayodhya Railway Station to commemorate the opening of Sri Ram Janam Bhoomi Temple.

In order to rescue his wife from the king of demons - Ravan, Sri Ram had to launch an assault on Lanka, which was encircled by the sea from all sides. To cross this enormous ocean, a bridge had to be built with extremely short lead times before any further action could be taken. The concept of a floating bridge was a novel yet extremely difficult undertaking. One day, Sri Ram and his younger brother Lakshmana stood on the wide ocean's shores. Sri Ram pointed towards a small squirrel.

Numerous powerful monkeys were transporting stones and other materials from all over to the construction site. Lakshman was amused to witness a small squirrel hopping in the water, rolling on the beach sand, and racing to the spot to shake the sand off its body on the section of the bridge that was still under construction among the buzzing activity. It was irritating monkeys carrying boulders to the site, as they had to watch out for the safety of the little squirrel. It appeared that the little squirrel, unaware of the seriousness of the situation, was having fun on the seashore.

Sri Ram instructed Hanuman to fetch the squirrel. When it was presented to him, he cradled it in his hand, gazing at it with deep affection. The squirrel, in turn, showed its reverence by folding its hands and closing its eyes.

"There goes that pesky squirrel, which keeps disrupting our work," remarked one of the monkeys.

Squirrel pleaded," Please let me continue! I also want to contribute to the construction of this bridge."

"You're just fooling around," retorted another monkey.

The squirrel protested. "Like the monkeys, I am also diligently placing sand between the stones to aid in the construction of the bridge. I am small and weak compared to these mighty monkeys, but this is the best I can do," the squirrel said with tears in its eyes.

The response of the squirrel humbled everyone around, and they were filled with gratitude. Sri Ram gently ran his finger over the body of the squirrel, showering it with affection and blessings. It's said that from that moment on, squirrels have stripes on their bodies.

The story teaches several morals:

Firstly, no task is insignificant; it's the intention behind the action that truly matters.

Secondly, true devotion doesn't require following prescribed rituals; sincerity in one's devotion is what counts.

Lastly, quietly carry out good deeds without seeking recognition, for ultimately, all actions are observed by a higher power.

STEPS ON THE PATH OF YOGA – FLOW DIAGRAM

Yoga of Gita can be summed up in the following steps:

Knowledge
I am neither mind nor body but soul.
Death is inevitable, and therefore, the world is temporary.
Difficulties and unfavourable conditions are unavoidable. Develop tolerance towards these
Don't look for happiness outside. Happiness is nothing but a natural state of mind. We only disturb it.
Kamana (lust) is the most formidable enemy of man. It never satiates. Self-restraint is a must to enjoy eternal bliss.

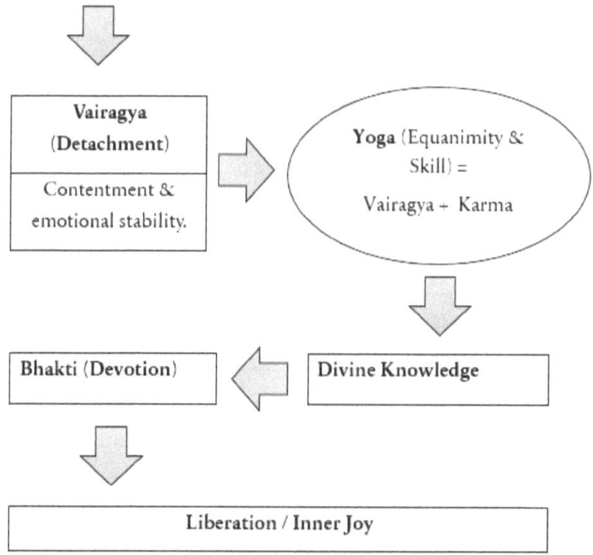

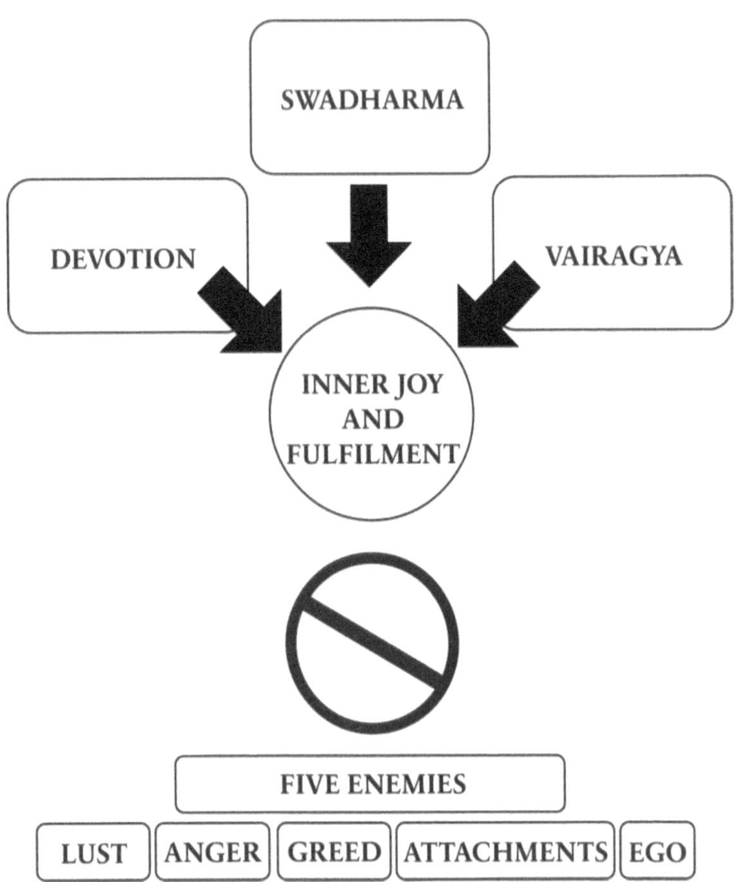
SWADHARMA
DEVOTION
VAIRAGYA
INNER JOY AND FULFILMENT
FIVE ENEMIES
LUST
ANGER
GREED
ATTACHMENTS
EGO

14.

THE SCIENCE OF YOGA

Sri Krishan simplified yoga and approached it from the point of view of *Nishkaam (without lust) Karma*. Another exclusive, deeper analysis of yoga has been carried out by Maharashi Patanjali, which covers the vastness of all aspects of yoga.

The definition of yoga in Patanjali's Yoga Sutra is:

"Yoga Chit Vritti Nirodh" (Patanjali vs. 2).

The Sanskrit word *'Nirodh'* can be translated as similar to – inhibit, prevent, check, control, cessation, remove, etc. The above verse gets clearer if seen in the continuation of the next verse:

"Tadha drushtu swarupe-avasthanam" (Patanjali vs. 3)

At that time, the seer is established in his own nature.

An analysis of these two verses together implies that the essence of yoga is to eliminate obstacles of *chit* and *vritti* to establish one's own nature.

There are some other complex Sanskrit language terms used in scriptures to describe these concepts. Many learned scholars on the subject have given their explanations of these, which in layman's language are defined as follows:

Mental Faculty - forms of *Anathakaran.*	
Buddhi	Intellect. Ability to discriminate (called *Vivek)*. It can be from current or past life learnings.
Manas	Receives information created by the senses from outside experiences. Awareness. Thinking without discrimination. Causes of *Raag (passions)* and *Davesh (aversions)*. All *Sankalp* (resolutions or decisions) and Vikalp (options) are in *Manas*.
Ahamkara	Sense of identity (which separates). It is not ego in this context.
Chitta	Sub Consciousness. Storehouse of all impressions.
Vritti	Thought waves and ripples
Samskara	Tendencies build due to continuous thought waves (Vritti) on Chitta.

In situations where *Manas* is the dominant aspect of life, individuals are guided by past experiences, whether enjoyable or repulsive. When *Buddhi* is dominant, then one uses intellect to decide the course of response or action, not merely based on the directions on *Manas*, which rely on memory of past experiences. *Chitta* is consciousness, which is away from the influence of *Manas, Budhi,* and *Ahamkar*. It is a reflection of Atman in the individual's body.

Vrttti leaves an imprint on *Chitta* like the waves do to the lake bed, then creates similar thought waves and creates *Samskara*. This process works both ways, like a cycle. The wrong or worldly impression due to *Ahamkara* can be corrected by modifying thought waves through practice in the various techniques of yoga. It is not controlling the mind or making it blank.

Once these *chitta-vrittis* (*Vritti* arising in *Chitta*) are addressed, then supreme consciousness shines through the body. The reliance of yoga is not on intellect (Buddhi) in the form of knowledge but on cleansing through disciplined practice to attain the natural state of *Chitta*.

Atman is outside the preview of thought waves; it is pure and free. Man can never know or realise *Atman* as long as it is associated with a false identity. The mind doesn't possess intelligence; it only reflects the borrowed intelligence of *Atman*. Patanjali analysis of cleansing doesn't work on *Ahamkar* or *Budhi* but on improving *Vritti* and then *Chitta* so that one can be established in pure consciousness.

It is not like the construction of a building that, once built, is available to use years later. *Vritti* keeps forming all the time.

Discipline of Yoga

The first verse of the Patanjali Yoga Sutra is *"Atha Yoganusashanam."*

This is the discipline of yoga, which means yoga is self-retrain and norms for the purification of *Chitta-Vritti* to establish one in a natural state through **continuous practice** and *vairagya* (Patanjali 1.12). Patanjali has formulated eight limbs of yoga, whereas Sri Krishan's ways are the simplified practice of *vairagya*, action, and devotion to address *Vritti* to establish in one's own nature. There are various ways to attain one goal.

Traditionally, there are four paths of yoga: Jana (Gyan) Yoga, Karma Yoga, Raj Yoga, and Bhakti Yoga. These paths appear to be different, but I support the school of thought that considers them all complementary to the supreme goal. In my understanding, The Gita strengthens this belief by emphasising the importance of knowledge, Karma, Bhakti, and touching upon Raja Yoga in subsequent chapters. One can choose to rely on either of the paths, but other paths provide the strength required for the overall practice.

Jana, Karma, and Bhakti got sufficient attention in the previous chapters. Raj Yoga is called the Royal Path—the way to administer the mind and body. This is the path of techniques like hatha yoga (often confused with overall yoga by beginners), meditation, and breathing exercise. Doctors also recommend these techniques to mitigate the impact of stress and a sedentary lifestyle. Patanjali described *Ashta*ng Yoga—the eight limbs of yoga—in the Yoga Sutra from vs. 2.29 to vs. 2.55.

15.

THE YOGA TOOL KIT

Yama and *Niyama,* which are part of *Ashtanga Yoga,* are important for peace. These are like the Ten Commandments for the spiritual path.

Yama consists of the following abstinences (prohibited actions):

Ahimsa (non-violence), *Satya* (truthfulness), *Asetheya* (not stealing and not missing what you don't have), *Bhramacharya* (continence, self-restraint, keeping in mind the bigger picture of *Bhraman* (universe)), *Aprigrha* (not taking what people give you, either appreciation or insult. Let it go!)

Niyama includes the following observances:

Shucha (physical and mental hygiene), *Santosha* (contentment), *Tapa* (to make mind and body strong), *Swadhyaya* (self study; observing mind and thoughts), and

Ishwara Pranidhaani (acceptance of divine will or devotion to God).

Maharishi Patanjali, at vs. 2.1 of the Patanjali Yoga Sutra, says that the preliminary steps towards the practice of yoga are:

- *Tapa*
- *Swadhaya* (Self-study)
- *Ishwara Pranidhaani* (acceptance of divine will or devotion to God).

'*Tapa*' carries a lot of significance in religious practices and yoga. '*Tapa*' is a Sanskrit word that signifies voluntary hardship or self-discipline. Austerity does convey its exact meaning. *Tapa* can be in any form, like following a daily ritual of prayer, pranayama, hatha yoga, meditation, fasting, etc., or a combination of any of these. Even getting up early in the morning, eating vegetarian food, fasting, etc. are also types of *tapa*. Similarly, performing duty (Swadharma) rather than sense pleasures, passions, or self-glorification is considered the highest form of *tapa*.

Sri Krishan's description in the Gita vs. 17.14 -17.19 clarifies *Tapa*.

"Worship of God, twice born, Guru (teacher) and wise: purity, simplicity, bhramcharya, and non-violence - these are tapa of the body. Words that don't agitate others are truthful, pleasant, and beneficial, and the study of scriptures is said to be the austerity of speech. Cheerfulness of mind, peaceful nature (gentleness), silence, self-restraint, and purity of emotion are tapa of mind. Tapa performed without seeking fruits and with supreme faith or

devotion is Satvik in nature, but to gain respect, honour, show off, and for transient and uncertain results is Rajsik in nature. Tapa performed with foolish determination through self-torture and with the intention to harm others is Tamsik in nature."

Determination:

Yoga requires repeated practice to master the skill. One among many chooses this path, and among those rare, one is able to achieve the supreme. It is impossible to reach such a state that one can be confident that he will never succumb to human instinct again. Strong determination and persistence are essential for returning to his practice after falling many times, as distractions due to inbuilt tendencies are bound to create obstacles now and then.

Knowledge of three modes of nature:

Mind and matter have three modes (called *gunn*):

- *Sattva:* goodness, light, purity, and freedom from sorrow.
- *Rajas:* passion, activity, and energy give birth to selfish desires and anger.
- *Tamas:* darkness, inertia, laziness, and ignorance.

The wise understand these three modes, which dominate nature and are the cause of all actions. Sattva uplifts, Rajas keeps him where he is, embroiled in day-to-day chase, and Tamas sinks him downwards. The same man decides and acts differently as per the dominant mode at that time in his mind. The wise transcend the influence of these three modes of nature. Knowing that these modes of nature influence all actions, a yogi realises God, which is above all these modes, and enters into union with him.

Discrimination (Vivek)

Sri Krishna counts nonviolence as one of the attributes of tapa of the body, despite the fact that throughout the Bhagavad-Gita, he strives to convince Arjun to pick up weapons and fight. This is just an example. One faces such contradictions several times. Either this or that? In everyday life, one encounters numerous choices at each step. Every step necessitates decision-making. Choices that are made today significantly impact the future. To progress towards the goal, it is essential to exercise discrimination in identifying and acting on the right course of action. Personal growth, in both spiritual and material aspects, requires developing the ability to make discerning choices in all aspects of life.

The power to discriminate is so important that it differentiates a fool from a wise person. It is essential to recognise and steer clear of *tamsik* and *rajsik* activities, including certain types of food, for holistic personal development. One must differentiate between what is illusory and what is real, the eternal and the temporary, and learn to make wise choices without being swayed by instincts. Accomplishing this task is demanding, requiring not just accurate knowledge but also intelligence and self-discipline to control sensory and ego impulses. Merely possessing knowledge is ineffective.

Tolerance towards the pair of opposites

Humans naturally seek pleasure and avoid pain. At the same time, difficulties are part of life. There is no option but to face challenges on this journey. There is no other way out but to be tolerant of them. Jesus, Sri Krishna, and Sri Ram encountered challenges in their lives.

Heat, cold, pleasure, and pain a person experiences due to the contact of senses with sense objects. These come and go and are inevitable, so be tolerant towards them. Wise men, who treat pleasure and pain alike and are not affected by them, become eligible for immortality. (BG 2.14 and 2.15).

The Gita mandates to bear pleasure and pain patiently. Not be elated in pleasure and tormented in pain. Pleasure and pain continue to make one feel good and worse, but a wise person should see them as transient in nature and stay calm in adversity.

Friendly and compassionate

The thoughts of hate, jealousy, and animosity are self-punishing. Patanjali Yoga Sutra vs. 1.33 states that the virtues that cultivate an undisturbed calmness of mind are:

- Friendliness (Maitre) towards the happy
- Compassion (Karuna) towards unhappy
- Delight or Joy (Mudita) for good
- Virtuous and indifference (Upeksha) towards wicked or evil

Sri Krishan also declares that one who does not possess malice for anyone, is friendly and compassionate to all, and acts in the same manner with friends and foes is dear to me.

Contentment

With contentment, one gains supreme happiness

(Patanjali vs. 2.42).

Cravings and desires push people to make continuous efforts without ever finding satisfaction. A Yogi, who focuses solely on following their true calling (Swadharma), distances themselves from the exhausting and frustrating rat race that others engage in. Living without desires does not equate to a boring life. Finding contentment does not imply being idle or avoiding challenges. Contentment is acceptance of any outcome as divine will. It is living with the belief that consequences stem from past or present actions (karma).

Moderation

Sri Krishan mandates that a yogi must be moderate in eating, sleeping, recreation, and work. This is an optimal way to live a balanced life out of the trap of lower instincts like attachments, ego, and passion. Moderation empowers a yogi to regulate their physical health, mental clarity, and emotional stability. The practice of yoga also mandates that one remain cautious of laziness as well as excessive recreation. A balanced life leads to inner peace, contentment, and overall happiness. Engaging in a perpetual pursuit inevitably leads to a state of restlessness and dissatisfaction. Consuming the right food in appropriate amounts and timings is a subtle science. Food not only profoundly affects physical health but also plays a crucial role in shaping the mind, which is the primary focus of spiritual practice.

Pranayama

'Breath is the link between body and mind.' – Srisri

There is complex biochemistry behind every living entity. Laymen observe it every day in the form of the use of medicine to cure various diseases.

By now, every educated person knows the impact exercise has on the body. However, breathing is gradually being recognised as another significant factor in the well-being of an individual. Breathing is a crucial phenomenon of the exchange of gases between the body and the environment, facilitating biochemistry work inside the body.

Emotions, or what is going on inside the mind, create modifications in the rhythm of breathing, which can be easily observed. The breath is short when one is angry or anxious, and the breath is slow and light when the mind is calm.

Engaging in breathing exercises directly calms the mind, alleviating negative emotions and restlessness. Pranayama – the breathing techniques or practice is a mix of the words *Prana* and *Ayama* – to regulate or lengthen. Pranayama removes blockages in energy channels that cause worry, tension, and conflict. It is the easiest approach to calm a restless mind, besides reducing the ageing process and boosting the immune system and overall health. The calmness and silence energise the mind and body and also prepare for a better experience in meditation.

Food

The body of a living being depends on food. Hindus thousands of years ago discovered the impact food has on the mind and advised dos and don'ts for improving quality of thought. Food also possesses *paranic* value. The Bhagavad Gita defines three types of food. *Satvik* food promotes longevity, intelligence, health, vigour, and cheerfulness. *Rajsik* foods are bitter, sour, salty, overly hot, pungent, and dry and cause suffering, grief, and sickness. Foods that are ill-cooked, not ripe, insipid, putrid, stale, unclean, impure, and left over are of *Tamasik* nature. The type of food consumed propels particular tendencies in men. Therefore, one who practices calmness and self-control needs to observe discipline to consume food to develop conducive thoughts.

Hatha Yoga

We have learned from a young age that a healthy mind resides in a healthy body. Hatha yoga is normally practiced as a form of physical fitness tool that has been gaining popularity after medical science established its benefits through scientific research. Hatha yoga is distinct from aerobics or cardiovascular exercise. During the period when Hatha yoga evolved, contemporary issues due to a sedentary lifestyle were not prevalent. Hatha yoga was developed as a subtle technique to integrate mind and body to stimulate spiritual energy. Therefore, it is also being medically prescribed to relax, calm the mind, and overcome mental weaknesses in the form of anxiety and restlessness. But all these benefits are by-products of Hatha yoga, whereas in actuality, it is a step towards yoga. Hatha Yoga comprises eighty-four positions (*asanas*), which are the outcome of the profound knowledge of ancient yogis and rishis developed to open up energy channels. The benefit of Hatha yoga multiplies when it is practiced with the right breathing pattern learned from a knowledgeable teacher.

Meditation

Meditation is a profound discovery for humans. It is the simplest but most wonderful gift one can give to himself. It nourishes the soul and is a remedy to subdue the senses, realise reality, improve understanding, and experience union with the supreme. Meditation is not the same as focus, but it is effortless. It is silence and a superior form of rest. Meditation is not controlling thoughts; it is a simple technique of pacifying the mind, which is always restless like a monkey and jumps from one thought to another. Meditation not only calms the wandering mind, providing relief, but also yields immense health benefits for the practitioner. Meditation has been accepted as essential for spiritual growth.

Meditation is bliss!

Ram, the four gatekeepers at the entrance of the empire of freedom are:

- Self-control
- Spirit of inquiry
- Contentment
- Good company

  - Rishi Vasistha's advice to Sri Ram in the Yog Vasishtha

16.

YOGA – WHY?

The Isha Upanishad, considered the first Upanishad, resonates deeply with me as its first two verses encapsulate the ideology essential for guiding a significant aspect of our lives.

"God envelops all that exists in this changing universe. Enjoy it through renunciation (tayag) without getting entangled in it. Wealth has never belonged to anyone.

Thus, performing actions, intend to live for a hundred years. Except for actions performed like this, there is no other way Karma will not cling to the soul."

God exists in everything in the universe. Keep enjoying it. But how? Through renunciation! And don't get entangled in it, as the universe is changing and wealth here doesn't belong to anyone. So don't let thoughts of ownership and possessiveness dominate your mind. One should enjoy life without getting bewildered, distracted, or living under any burden because everything is changing in this universe. Sometimes too much seriousness around religion and the righteous approach makes enjoyment appear like a sin, which is contradictory to the right way prescribed in the Isha Upanishad. Enjoyment is a natural part of life and should be embraced without guilt, but in the prescribed way.

The second verse is to desire to live for a hundred years, which also means that one can live for a hundred years but not forever. Simultaneously, it guides individuals to engage in work with enthusiasm. But how? With consciousness of God in everything, without greed or for ownership, through renunciation (*Vairagya*), so that Karma doesn't cling to the soul and man remains free of *Karma-Bandan*.

This is what yoga is. A technique for holistic living, peace, overcoming fears and conflicts, fulfilling duties towards oneself, family, relatives, and society, and addressing both spiritual and material aspects. It was evident that a war of such magnitude would end with the elimination of one of the sides. No other circumstances could be more serious, as the outcome was a question of life and death. Sri Krishan taught yoga to Arjun amidst a battleground, which denotes its relevance for handling even the most challenging situations of one's life. At the same time, the skill is also valid in everyday life. The choice of background in war is also an indicator that one has to make hard decisions during the struggle in life, and yoga is the way to take up challenges.

Why should one follow yoga?

Besides the gains in terms of peace or tranquilly, some of the other benefits of Krishna's yoga in day-to-day life can be summed up as follows:

Cost of effort

Sri Krishan introduces the path of yoga in Chapter 2, Verse 39, with the reasoning that no effort ever goes to waste on this path and there is no failure. This is clearly logical. Action is the central theme of yoga. A Yogi engages in work similar to that of an ordinary person. Following karma yoga does not result in any materialistic disadvantages.

Emotional Intelligence

Any smart person knows that staying calm or not getting worked up is the path to success. One facet of emotional stability is the ability to accept ups and downs, success and loss, with grace. However, tolerance is not a natural disposition. This needs to be developed over time. Another dimension is containing an instant reaction. The man is designed to react automatically in the face of a threat. The same chemistry operates under emotional stress, resulting in unanticipated alterations, unpleasant statements, and physical or verbal fights. Reaction is natural; however, some people have a short fuse, whereas others can respond calmly to the same situation.

It is not restricted to negative reactions; emotional reactions are also portrayed via excessive generosity, love, and acts of kindness, which are cherished, but sometimes in real life, one regrets decisions made due to overwhelming emotions later on. Who hasn't heard the advice not to look at things or think from the heart? Aside from the inbuilt system, there are a number of other factors that influence our response to a situation, such as the importance of a specific outcome, the nature of the threat, ego, and so on.

Yoga is about achieving mental balance. This is similar to the modern concept of emotional intelligence, which is acknowledged as an important leadership quality. It provides us with more control over our emotions and allows us to make better judgements in both personal and professional situations.

Bondages of Action (*Karmabandhan*)

As one grows older, he begins to realise that not everything that is desired offers the anticipated delight or contentment. Furthermore, unexpected or undesirable results can sometimes be more advantageous.

The outcome may not always be a direct result of immediate actions. The theory of karma is based on the concept that whatever good or bad happens to a person is an effect of his karmas, which are not only confined to this life but also to previous lives. Karmas are not limited to actions but also to the intention behind the action.

Each act of karma causes ripples. The reason for Arjun's worry was justified. To win the battle, he had to commit the sin of killing his cousins, teacher, and grandfather. According to the theory of karma, one must face the consequences of his actions. Yet, the Gita explains that practicing karma with yoga does not lead to karmic bondage.

"Regarding victory and defeat, gain and loss, pleasure and pain as the same, get ready to fight. By fighting in this way, you will not incur sin." (BG 2:38)

"By using the intelligence of yoga, one can overcome the positive and negative effects of karma; hence, engage in karma with the skill of yoga." (BG 2:50)

Protection from fear

Miserable are those who work for results. (BG 2.49). Little effort on this path protects from fear (BG 2.40). Insecurity is one of the major reasons for misery. Yoga is a change of attitude that obviates the very reason for fear, which is necessary for calmness and serenity. Most of the time, men engrossed in day-to-day activities remain in the grip of fear of loss in one form or another. On the path of yoga, when failures and disrespect get the same treatment as success or honour, there is no scope for fear. What matters is the performance of *swadharma*, which gives a spiritual strength for tolerance for negatives in the pair opposites, i.e., disrespect, failure, pain, misery, etc. Detachment (Vairagya) leads to freedom from fear and, consequently, leads to joy. Renunciation, *swadharma,* and surrender to the divine also free man from the mental burden associated with actions.

Clarity of mind

The multitude of choices often leaves individuals feeling lost and working without clear personal life goals for the future. There are many possibilities arising out of permutation and combination as to what should be done in a situation. So many factors are beyond control and any anticipation. Thinking is endless, and therefore the mind fails to find rest in figuring out outcomes or situations in the future. This confusion engages the mind in endless thoughts and drains energy to act. Unless one follows the simple path taught by Sri Krishan, life becomes pathetic.

When work is for *swadharma,* there is no dilemma about the actions one should perform. This frees man from the ambiguity and confusion of whether he has selected the right course of action or not. This ultimately leads to a sense of peace and fulfilment.

Health

Medical research has confirmed that inner peace directly impacts the physical well-being of individuals. Conditions such as depression, heart disease, and other mental disorders are attributed to stress, overthinking, negative thoughts, and frustrations. Work itself is not the source of stress; rather, anxiety and fear are the negative outcomes. Scientific research has proven that stress is the prime cause of distortion in body fluids or chemistry inside the human body.

Productivity

There is no one who is so blessed that he will always succeed and will never face failure in life. It is quite easy to say, "Stop worrying and get back to work. Leave the results to him." But actual life is quite challenging. Due to misfortune, mistakes, inadequate handling, and various other reasons, there can be losses and, in certain cases, disasters. What is the option left for a person? He has to gather courage, overcome any negative emotions, and start afresh. There is no guarantee that he will succeed this time, but in order to succeed or survive, that is the only possibility. Action for a yogi is the foremost dharma to be followed in all circumstances.

Yoga only mandates relinquishing attachment to outcomes. The discipline of yoga helps a practitioner maintain inner balance during success and resilience to bounce back from failures. Since Yogi works without feverishness, his actions are more productive in a normal course too.

17.

CHALLENGES ON THE PATH OF YOGA

The availability of books, discourses on television, cassettes, and now the social media revolution have enhanced the reach of all sorts of information. Earlier, one had to travel to faraway places to be with a master to gain this knowledge. Though being with a master is still the best way to grasp the minute hidden meanings in profound knowledge, technology has helped in a big way. Still, in spite of repetitive reading, listening, and knowing, it remains difficult to practice these learnings in normal, day-to-day life. Why?

Search for Happiness: Mindless is restless, and craving

The biggest disease of mankind is the search for happiness and more happiness. This has further aggravated with the introduction of more and more modes and venues of so-called fun or essential requirements for a perceived good life. Besides the age-old attraction for status, liquor, opposite sex, and property, today there are a variety of foods, expensive gadgets, glamorous household items, places to visit, restaurants to try, etc. Only a few wise people, after frustration or understanding the pitfalls of worldly pleasure, adopt the path of spiritualism for happiness.

The desires and cravings never die, and spiritualism has again become the route to fill those instincts for many. People even walk on the path of spirituality with the expectation of ecstasy. Nothing changes until the perception of what is happy and successful rises above ordinary understanding. The spiritual path is very subtle. It requires a deep inner journey over a long period of time to gain the correct understanding. And only after experiencing its profound impact on their lives can one truly appreciate the power of yoga. Till such time, the higher truth appears like a mere outdated theory.

Ahankara

Self-pride and pride are confusing terms with very thin lines of difference. Self-esteem is another dimension of it. In spite of knowing the futility of Ego or *Ahankara*, control over such thoughts is not easy. Rooting out 'Karta-Bhav', which means working with the notion that I am the doer, is an essential ingredient of the concept of Karma Yoga, which can't be ignored at any step.

Attachments

Attachments to people, possessions, or even a particular subject matter are natural, and it is very challenging to break free from them. The idea that we originate from infinity and will return to it helps us understand the temporary nature of everything. Surrender, arising from such higher thoughts, can only bring relief to the soul trapped in the whirlpool of attachment and ego.

Yogi is rare

"Hardly among thousand men, one strives for perfection, and those who strive and succeed, hardly one knows Me in real truth."
(BG 7.3)

Yoga is not the path adopted by a large number of people. Yogi is rare. He is different from the crowd, as most of the people remain victims of desires, attachments, or are deprived of the realisation of inner joy. They continue to look outside for happiness. First, only very few people want to improve and work for perfection, and secondly, hardly one of those realises the truth. That is why one comes across cheats pretending to be masters in every religion who make false claims that they are blessed with divine vision.

Yoga is a discipline, and one rarely gets the right inspiration for it. ***The Yogi primarily walks the path alone.*** He is different from the masses, who continue to live normal, rollercoaster lives.

Osho said that there are no herds of Buddhas. After centuries, one Buddha (an enlightened person) is born.

Man is a social animal, so his surroundings have an impact on him. We observe this clearly as parents of growing children. But we fail to see, to an extent, the same in ourselves. We all want social acceptance. We spend so much mental energy on the validation of people who matter to us. We continue to tune ourselves for it without realising that those around us are also imperfect. We want to be appreciated by those who are looking for meaningfulness in their lives and living with their own insecurities.

Though social norms always encourage higher values and moral conduct, the dilemma is often about truly following them. The conflict may be the acceptability of some set of values for survival or commercial reasons. Everyone talks about it but does not necessarily follow these values. Yogi has to monitor inside; he has to find the right beacon to navigate him to his goal amid a myriad of distractions and misleading information in the name of religion. He has to face his inner voice, which may question his selection based on socially acceptable standards. Instead of pursuing the criteria that those around him are following, is he wasting time and energy? Is he easy-going or irresponsible? Such a man may cause worry for family members.

Birds of the same feather flock together. But a true Yogi is alone. He might not find genuine inspiration or companionship among the masses in religious places. Steering through this journey alone poses significant challenges. Locating an authentic and appropriate role model may prove challenging at times.

Remedy

Many individuals, like myself, frequently make resolutions for improvement, only to see them fade away with time, leading life back to familiar patterns.

Arjun also felt the same way while listening to the teachings. So, he asked Sri Krishan. *"Mind is restless. I don't perceive the sustainability of this yoga in the form of equanimity. The mind is as difficult to control as the wind. It is unsteady, turbulent, tenacious, and powerful."* (BG 6.33 & 6:34)

Even if all other negative virtues like greed, lust, attachments, etc. are ignored for a moment, anger and ego are so dominant that they appear from nowhere and take over. There is always the possibility of distraction, even after spending a long time in true spiritual life. As mentioned earlier, lust (*Kamna,* or strong desires) is the most formidable enemy *(BG 3.43)* and senses sway the mind, like wind in a storm taking away a boat *(BG 2.67).* Each person's personality comprises intricate layers that vary. Individuals harbour latent tendencies stemming from their actions from current and past lives that continue to influence their instincts. The spiritual growth is not only gradual but also like the game of snake and ladder. Many times, after making remarkable progress, one falls from that state at the spur of the moment due to the whirlpool of *Maya.* These are malware, which overrides all firewalls and takes over the system.

Sri Krishan acknowledges the restless and hard-to-control nature of the mind but explains that it can be managed **through consistent practice and cultivating dispassion** (*BG 6.35*). Yoga is a lifelong practice, not one-time learning or achievement. It is against our normal instincts. However, the practice (*sadhana*) is the only way out. Yoga is difficult to achieve for those who have not subdued their mind. For those who are ceaselessly striving to gain perfection, it can be easily attained through practice. Practice with determination and perseverance is key to success in attaining the state of yoga.

Patanjali also echoed the same message of Gita in verse 1.12:

Practice and non-attachment are the means of restraining Vritti.

Patanjali further defines practice as a repeated effort to follow discipline to gain perfection. He emphasises that practice has to be cultivated for a long time, uninterruptedly, with sincere devotion, to make it firmly grounded.

> *The mind is difficult to conquer, but yoga can be achieved only through regular practice, self-restraint, and vairagya (dispassion).*

Am I a Yogi? – A Checklist

	☐ Do I rely on INNER JOY or chase happiness?
Vairagya	☐ Am I happy within myself? ☐ Am I ready to accept any outcome? ☐ Does the challenge of the world move me, or do I just look at these like witnesses (*Sakshi*)? ☐ How easily do I come back to my natural state of mind, unaffected by any event? ☐ Am I self-obsessed or consider myself a miniscule being in this universe?
Karma	☐ Am I doing what should be done? ☐ Are my actions propelled by a sense of duty, ego, or sense-pleasure? ☐ Are my actions motivated by fruits or by a sense of dharma?
Bhakti	☐ Do I believe every moment that everything dwells in God? ☐ Do I see the same Lord in others as I do in myself? ☐ Am I living in gratitude right now? ☐ Do I surrender to the will of God after making my efforts?

Conclusion

This book starts by exploring the hidden and often overlooked natural bliss that is otherwise available to everyone. Quick-fix solutions provide temporary relief from mental noise, but lasting joy remains out of reach due to life's multifaceted nature. Practicing Krishna's yoga principles addresses life's complexities. More than theory, it offers a practical path to enhance life quality. It's not a religion but a practical technique to genuinely improve life.

The Bhagavad Gita is a profound source of wisdom and insight. A thorough reading shows the challenge of summarising or commenting on its content. This work aims to distil the essence of the Gita's teachings as a reminder to find joy. Nothing can substitute the bliss of reading the Gita and the knowledge it emanates in every stanza. Reading the Bhagavad Gita repeatedly is such a bliss, as it allows one to absorb the wisdom that this sacred text radiates in each verse.

Ultimately, the Bhagavad Gita serves as a tool for individuals leading ordinary lives, extending its relevance beyond just saints. Its true wonder lies in accurate comprehension and constant application. In conclusion, the core message of this book is to recognise equanimity of mind as the goal of yoga and explore the knowledge and practice required for it.